World Order and Local Disorder

PUBLISHED FOR THE
CENTER OF
INTERNATIONAL STUDIES, PRINCETON UNIVERSITY
A LIST OF OTHER CENTER PUBLICATIONS APPEARS
AT THE BACK OF THE BOOK

WORLD ORDER
AND LOCAL DISORDER

The United Nations and
Internal Conflicts

BY LINDA B. MILLER

PRINCETON, NEW JERSEY

PRINCETON UNIVERSITY PRESS

1967

FOR MY FAMILY

Acknowledgments

IT IS A PLEASURE to acknowledge the generosity and encouragement of those who have helped to make this book possible. The manuscript was prepared for publication in the stimulating and congenial atmosphere of Princeton University's Center of International Studies, where I served as Research Associate in 1966-1967. I am especially indebted to Klaus Knorr, Director of the Center, for support. The final text benefited from his careful reading and the critical judgment of other Center members, particularly Leon Gordenker, Richard A. Falk, Harry Eckstein, Gabriella R. Lande, and Harold Sprout. Ruth B. Russell, then of the Brookings Institution, provided many useful suggestions that enhance the discussion of detailed case studies.

While at Columbia, I received helpful comments from the late Otto Kirchheimer. My undergraduate tutor and friend, Stanley Hoffmann, sustained me through the difficult rights of passage to the doctorate with uncommon loyalty. I would like to thank Phoebe Morrison and Thomas P. Peardon, my senior colleagues in the Department of Government at Barnard College, for their interest during our association.

The secretarial services of Mrs. Shirley Lerman and later the Princeton Center were exemplary. William McClung of Princeton University Press cheerfully and patiently answered all questions during the editing and printing stages. Dorothy Hollmann was a vigorous and painstaking editor whose sense of style greatly improved the final text.

The book is dedicated to my family in appreciation for their devoted concern throughout the years of research and writing.   L.B.M.

December 1966, Princeton, N.J.

Contents

World Order and Local Disorder

ABBREVIATIONS

ANC	Congolese National Army
FLN	Algerian Front of National Liberation
GPRA	Provisional Government of the Algerian Republic
OAS	Organization of American States
OAU	Organization of African Unity
ONUC	United Nations Operation in the Congo
UMHK	Union Minière de Haut Katanga
UNCI	United Nations Commission for Indonesia
UNEF	United Nations Emergency Force
UNFICYP	United Nations Force in Cyprus
UNOGIL	United Nations Observer Group in Lebanon
UNSCOB	United Nations Special Committee on the Balkans
UNYOM	United Nations Yemen Observation Mission

Introduction

THE increasing prevalence of internal disorders in the contemporary international system poses vexing problems for both political theorists and policy-makers. For theorists, difficulties arise from the fact that methods of investigation deemed suitable for examining other political phenomena are of little value in evolving a theory of internal violence.[1] Policy-makers, charged with formulating and executing sustained or ad hoc policies representing national or international interests may, like theorists, find traditional concepts suitable for international wars inapplicable to internal conflicts defying easy categorization.

Some scholars, confronted with a bewildering array of cases, have attempted to blur the distinction between various types of contemporary internal violence by using the term "internal war."[2] Although this term is used widely in the growing literature devoted to investigating the social, economic, political, and psychological aspects of contemporary civil strife,[3] it is not wholly adequate for scholarly inquiry. Many significant internal disorders, for example the recurring violence in the former Belgian Congo, are not "wars." "Internal war" is

[1] Harry Eckstein (ed.), *Internal War: Problems and Approaches* (New York: Free Press of Glencoe, 1964), p. 6.

[2] *Ibid.*, p. 3. For example, Eckstein cites 1,200 instances of "internal war" as reported in the *New York Times* in the period 1946-1959 (including civil wars, guerrilla wars, internal rioting, local terrorism, coups d'etat).

[3] See for example, George Modelski, *The International Relations of Internal War*, Center of International Studies Research Monograph No. 9 (Princeton: 1961); Cyril E. Black and Thomas P. Thornton (eds.), *Communism and Revolution* (Princeton: Princeton University Press, 1964); and James Rosenau (ed.), *International Aspects of Civil Strife* (Princeton: Princeton University Press, 1964).

rendered still less precise for purposes of analysis by its occasional use to describe a particular type of ostensibly civil conflict.[4] For these reasons, in the present study the terms "internal conflicts," "internal violence," and "internal disorders" will be used in preference to "internal wars."

The inadequacy of the term "internal war" is but one problem plaguing social scientists who would investigate the phenomenon of intrastate violence. The difficulties encountered in delimiting, analyzing, and classifying internal conflicts persist despite greater attention to the significance of these disorders in recent years.

Inquiry into internal disorders remains in a "pretheoretical" stage. As Eckstein argues, it is necessary to develop "descriptive categories in terms of which the basic features of internal wars can be identified, in terms of which their nuances and broader features can be depicted in general structural concepts, classes (or types) constructed, and resemblances of cases to one another or to types can be accurately assessed."[5] Only after such categories have been established will social scientists begin to comprehend the preconditions of internal violence, the courses such disorders take, and the long-term consequences of their evolution.

Attempts to develop convincing categories continue. One scholar seeking to classify the varied range of colonial wars, post-colonial internal conflicts, proxy wars, and other forms of intrastate violence suggests that these disorders be differentiated according to the objectives of the insurgents, the duration of the conflict, or the type

[4] See for example, Roger Hilsman, "Internal War: The New Communist Tactic," in Franklin Mark Osanka (ed.), *Modern Guerrilla Warfare* (New York: Free Press of Glencoe, 1962), pp. 452-463.

[5] Eckstein, p. 23.

of violence displayed. Lincoln Bloomfield takes the degree of foreign intervention as the starting point for analyzing various types of internal conflicts. He ranks them on a scale from "basically internal disorders" (for example, the 1953 East German uprising) to "externally abetted internal instability" (the 1962 Yemeni civil war and others) and finally, "externally created or controlled internal instability" (the 1948 Communist putsch in Czechoslovakia).[6] Difficult questions of interpretation arise when a theorist is asked to rank the complex disorders in the former Indochina along Bloomfield's scale, to give but one example. Statements of various national policy-makers concerned with the continuing violence in South Vietnam reflect conflicting assessments of the degree of external involvement and direction in the Southeast Asian conflict. Contemporary internal disorders are volatile in their evolution. They may originate as "basically internal" and become "externally abetted" or "controlled" over a period of time. Protracted conflicts in a single political or geographical entity, such as South Vietnam, may be classified by some writers or participants as "basically internal" and by others, at the same time, as "externally created." Problems of classification increase as detached observers or policy-makers attempt to make clear distinctions between genuinely internal conflicts and international conflicts.

Bloomfield's categories, while helpful in some respects, are not exhaustive, as the author himself acknowledges.[7] They run the risk of being too rigid to deal with elusive political phenomena and too dependent upon subjective interpretations to permit completely

[6] Lincoln Bloomfield, *International Military Forces* (Boston: Little Brown and Company, 1964), pp. 28-30.
[7] *Ibid.*, p. 28.

5

satisfactory distinctions among cases.[8] But similar objections may be raised against any other classification scheme. Academic study of contemporary internal disorders is in an early stage; published works necessarily reflect the difficulties inherent in finding acceptable criteria for distinguishing conflicts characterized by diversity and complexity.

Categories useful for analyzing internal conflicts from one perspective may not be useful for other purposes. Thus the present study, the first concerned with the role of the United Nations in contemporary internal conflicts, employs categories chosen for their value in assessing the Organization's record. The writer does not suggest that these categories are adequate for a theoretical approach to the international relations of internal violence. It may be argued that the classifications "colonial wars," "internal conflicts involving a breakdown in law and order," and "proxy wars and internal conflicts involving charges of external aggression or subversion" are not mutually exclusive. To be sure, in the Indonesian, Algerian, and Angolan cases, as well as in the Congo, Cyprus, and Dominican disorders, charges of "aggression" were brought before U.N. councils. Similarly, the recurring violence in the former Indochinese states has colonial and post-colonial roots. But it may be said that in the Organization's consideration of a particular disorder or series of disorders in one political

---

[8] Bloomfield places the immediate post-independence violence in the Congo in the category of "externally created or controlled internal instability" on grounds that "the hasty and unprepared withdrawal of Belgian power and authority" was a critical factor (*ibid.*, p. 30). Equally convincing evidence could be presented in favor of placing the disorders of July 1960–February 1961 in Bloomfield's first or second categories. Similarly, later periods of the Congo's internal violence might be placed in one of several categories.

entity a major characteristic has emerged. The cases are arranged according to the major characteristic of the conflict as it manifested itself during the period of U.N. concern. The chapters are organized according to the broad types of internal disorder with which the United Nations has dealt rather than according to procedures adopted by the Organization in particular cases. The efficacy of U.N. procedures—debate, resolution, investigation, observation, and peace-keeping—is assessed in the concluding chapter.

The literature on international organization includes numerous detailed studies of the functions and powers of U.N. organs and many examples of case studies. Other writers have discussed many of the conflicts considered in the present study, yet prior analyses of important disorders including those in the Congo have tended to stress limited aspects, such as the United Nations' use of force. It is hoped that the present work may help to bridge the gap between theoretical considerations of internal violence as a social phenomenon and empirical studies of international organization as a structural component of the international system. The urgency of the issues posed by internal conflicts for the international society makes scholarly neglect of the role of international institutions especially unfortunate.

Since the United Nations is a political institution concerned with the maintenance of international peace and security, it is important to clarify the interests of the Organization in internal conflicts. It is also necessary to examine the legal and political factors that have limited the Organization's effectiveness in dealing with internal conflicts judged to threaten international peace and security. Among the questions investigated are the following: To what extent has the United Nations served the interests of parties favoring the status quo or change in particular cases? To what extent has U.N. involvement served the principles of legitimacy and self-determination? What factors have influenced the choice of procedures adopted in each case? What trends of Charter usage and interpretation have developed in U.N. practice? In what ways has the increase in membership affected the Organization's response to various types of internal conflict? Does U.N. practice reveal a consistent approach to any particular type of internal conflict? What roles have regional organizations played in internal conflicts the United Nations has considered?

In Chapter 1, the political importance of internal disorders to the new states, to the superpowers, and to other nations is outlined. The sources of a U.N. concern for conflicts not mentioned in the Organization's Charter are explained. In Chapter 2, the Indonesian, Algerian, and Angolan cases are analyzed in order to reveal the significant features of colonial wars and the similarities and differences in the United Nations' approach to these disorders at different times in the Organization's history. In Chapter 3, the Congo, Cyprus, and Dominican cases are discussed with special reference to the consequences resulting from the need of the United Nations or particular member states to select, among competing groups or factions, candidates to perform the order-giving functions of government. In Chapter 4, the Organization's responses to a diversified series of intrastate conflicts including those in Greece, Guatemala, Hungary, Lebanon, Yemen, Laos, and Vietnam are assessed. Possible reasons for differences in the character of the United Nations' participation are advanced. In Chapter 5, the questions posed in the introduction are reconsidered in the light of Chapters 1-4, and implications for the United Nations' future responses are suggested.

CHAPTER I

The Nature of Internal Conflicts
and the Bases of International Concern

THE high incidence of intrastate violence expresses the revolutionary character of the contemporary international system. Internal disorders, whether in the form of armed insurrections, bloodless military coups, uprisings against colonial domination, or factional struggles for governmental power, reflect major influences in world politics: the cold war in its military, political, ideological, and psychological aspects; the transition from colonial administration to new regimes; and the uncertain balance induced by nuclear technology. It is not coincidental that countries in the less-industrialized geographical sectors of Asia, Latin America, Africa, and the Middle East are experiencing internal conflicts involving complex combinations of actual and potential violence. Despite enormous differences in political traditions or cultural development, the process of economic modernization these countries are now experiencing creates social and political upheaval and invites violent or subviolent civil strife.

Nevertheless, internal disorders are an old, if not always well-understood, feature of world politics. No major power—East or West—has achieved a unified governmental structure without severe internal disorders at some point in its history. It is necessary to delineate more clearly the nature of contemporary internal violence in order to understand the concerns of international organizations in these conflicts, for different kinds of internal violence create different kinds of international concerns and these concerns may involve the United Nations or competitive national interventions outside the U.N. structure. Contemporary international organization, in the form of the United Nations and regional bodies, offers alternatives to strictly national interventions in internal disorders. The process whereby these conflicts may be internationalized is no longer confined to the individual or collective actions of incumbents, insurgents, or foreign states with vested interests.

The development of the United Nations as a political institution has extended the parameters of external involvement in internal conflicts. Country A, seeking to replace the incumbent government of Country B with a regime more favorable to its own political or social views, may, with ideas or matériel, instigate or abet violence in Country B. Incumbents or insurgents in Country B may solicit overt foreign military or economic assistance. These patterns of external involvement are not new. But the growth of international machinery capable of diplomatic or physical intervention or interposition between insurgents and incumbents is a new feature of the international system.

The Dimensions of Internal Violence and the Policies of Third Parties

The "developing areas," a general term describing diversified geographical regions, contain societies susceptible to colonial wars and to post-colonial civil strife, proxy aggressions, or subversion from outsiders. While the sheer variety of the disorders to be analyzed in subsequent chapters may appear to preclude viable generalizations, common features of internal violence in modernizing countries as different from one another as

Cyprus, Yemen, Indonesia, the Dominican Republic, and Algeria may be discerned. For internal violence may be employed to secure political change when previously legitimate means of effecting change have broken down or when the goals of dissident groups cannot be realized via legitimate means.[1] Revolutions, civil wars, coups, or mere threats of force attest to issues of policy or ideology; disagreements over foreign policy, constitutional, ethnic, racial, or economic questions may spark violence that generates new issues for domestic participants and outsiders.[2] If the social and economic demands made upon governments are not satisfied, internal violence may erupt in states governed by military leaders, by civilian authorities, or by traditional oligarchs. As Lucian Pye argues, nation-building and insurgency are closely linked: the lack of a basic national consensus about the means and ends of government may raise doubts as to the legitimacy of the formal government in power. Bureaucratic inefficiencies may call into question the capacity of the ruling groups to govern.[3] Nation-building is not a political task confined to new states emerging from colonialism; nation-building is a continuous responsibility for governments with established political traditions and economic bases confronting change. Thus the problems facing Greece after World War II or the Dominican Republic after years of dictatorship and military rule are those of nation-building.

Special political hazards accompany decolonization, often the first step in nation-building, as the Indonesian,

[1] Cyril E. Black, in Black and Thornton, pp. 7-12ff.
[2] *Ibid.*, pp. 9-12.
[3] Lucian Pye, in Eckstein, pp. 158, 164.

12

Algerian, and Angolan cases illustrate. Equally precarious is the stage at which indigenous groups attempt to govern after the initial transfer of power is completed, as the Congo and Cyprus conflicts reveal. When disorder erupts in a colonial territory, a post-independence state, or an established nation, the course violence will assume cannot be plotted with certainty; internal disorders create policy choices for incumbent regimes and for other states seeking to shore up or topple the economic and territorial status quo. National, regional, or multilateral decision-making activity, separately or in combination, may be required to formulate a solution to a particular disorder. A diversity of methods and approaches is possible, and the non-use of U.N. or other formal machinery may be as consequential as the use of U.N. or other investigating, mediating, or ad hoc peace-keeping devices.

Indirect aggression rather than external attack has become the familiar mode for states wishing to penetrate the physical boundaries of other states. But internal conflicts, like interstate conflicts, serve other than military purposes for third-party states who become involved. The series of far-ranging competitions between the two superpowers on the one hand, and between the leading Communist powers on the other, must have a geographical arena. The developing nations whose political stabilities are so fragile, whose loyalties are so fluid, are the logical targets. Thus the political importance of contemporary internal disorders, with roots in problems of modernization and nation-building, is related to the national policy aspirations of the Soviet Union, China, and the United States. In varying degrees, the attitudes of policy-makers of these states to-

13

ward modernization and nation-building in developing countries are linked to domestic priorities as well as to foreign policy objectives. But the public statements of Soviet, Chinese, and American leaders indicate a shared awareness of the potentialities of internal violence for extending the national influence of third parties in "the third world."[4]

Revolution, occupying a central place in traditional Marxism-Leninism, plays a dynamic role in Russian relations with developing countries. The thrust of Moscow's effort, decreed publicly at the twentieth Party Congress, is directed toward two interrelated goals: the protection of Russian security and the establishment of Communist power in the third world.[5] Expressed doctrinally, internal violence is the last stage in the class struggle leading to the seizure of power. Communist take-over is conceived in progressive stages: first, detachment from the West (Egypt, Iraq, Ceylon); second, formation of transitory national democracies (Cuba, Guinea, Ghana, Mali, Indonesia); and, finally, direct control (North Vietnam, North Korea).[6] The successful pattern of take-over in Eastern Europe, accomplished with the direct participation of Soviet troops, is not a practicable model for Soviet penetration into Latin America, Africa, Asia, or the Middle East. The Soviets

---

[4] The interests of other states in extending national influence in countries experiencing internal disorder are also apparent, often in regional contexts, as the Yemen and Congo disorders illustrate. In the present loose bipolar system, the interests and aspirations of the United States, the Soviet Union, and China are central, but by no means exclusive. For additional discussion, see Andrew Scott "Internal Violence as an Instrument of Cold Warfare," in Rosenau, pp. 154-169, and Karl Deutsch and Morton A. Kaplan, "The Limits of International Coalitions," *ibid.*, pp. 170-185.

[5] Thomas P. Thornton, in Black and Thornton, pp. 247ff.

[6] *Ibid.*, pp. 248ff.

have learned that poor timing may render otherwise successful infiltration ineffective, even when incumbent governments are hopelessly inept. Among the reasons for the Communists' failure to capture control in fifteen or twenty target countries are an unwillingness to escalate the level of violence, an inability to combat preponderant American power, plus difficulty in translating nationalist sentiment for change into sympathy for Communism, especially among reformist military groups.[7]

The personal experience of Chinese Communist leaders in a protracted civil war has provided Maoist political theorists with a program and rationale for the support of "national liberation movements" in developing countries.[8] According primary attention to assisting the armed overthrow of "imperialism" and "feudalism," Peking officials strive to establish relations with Asian, African, and Latin American countries that enhance Chinese prestige at the expense of better relations with the United States.[9] Features of the system of nation-states constitute obstacles to the attainment of Chinese goals, Tang Tsou and Morton Halperin argue. Nationalism, a force Mao exploited in his struggle for conquest in China, may turn against the Chinese when developing countries engaged in internal violence come to regard the Chinese advocacy and use of military force in international relations as dangerous. Tactics employed by the Chinese in their own internal conflict may be resented by other states when Chinese revolutionary strat-

[7] Cyril E. Black, in *ibid.*, p. 417.

[8] For a detailed discussion, see Tang Tsou and Morton H. Halperin, "Mao-Tse-Tung's Revolutionary Strategy and Peking's International Behavior," *American Political Science Review*, LIX (March 1965), 80-99.

[9] *Ibid.*, p. 82.

egy is projected abroad.[10] In incidents of internal violence in developing countries Soviet and Chinese leaders have supported policies whose effects on the international system as a whole are destabilizing; but Soviet unwillingness to accept the risks of thermonuclear war gives its over-all strategy, whatever tactics it employs in particular situations, a more conservative cast than Communist Chinese revolutionary fervor.[11]

Historically, Louis Halle notes, the United States has felt obligated to promote "civic virtue in [other] countries, approving or rejecting their governments, condemning such domestic activities as violate the principles that we uphold within our own society."[12] In contrast to the doctrinal aspirations of the Communist states, the United States has elaborated no schemata of "take-over." Yet in no sense is the interest of U.S. policy-makers in internal disorders less intense than that of their Soviet or Chinese counterparts. American attitudes toward internal instabilities reveal a greater predilection for the status quo as opposed to revolutionary change, in keeping with the U.S. position as a "satisfied" world economic and military leader.[13] Ac-

[10] *Ibid.*, p. 98. See also A. Doak Barnett, *Communist China and Asia* (New York: Random House, 1960), chaps. 4-7, pp. 65-172.

[11] Bloomfield, pp. 31-32.

[12] Louis Halle, *The New Republic*, October 24, 1964, p. 18.

[13] Bloomfield, p. 30. Nevertheless, as Richard Falk points out, the interests of the superpowers in "stability" is an interest stressing the desirability of extending and defending a sphere of influence of one major grouping of states at the expense of the other. Thus the United States opposes "stability" in the Sino-Soviet sphere of influence while it endorses it elsewhere. Similarly, the Soviet Union seeks to maintain a favorable status quo in Eastern Europe and to stimulate change in Africa, Latin America, and Asia that may enhance its prestige in those regions. See Richard A. Falk, "Historical Tendencies, Modernizing and Revolutionary Nations, and the International Legal Order," *Howard Law Review*, VIII (Spring 1962), 128-151.

knowledgment by U.S. officials of the shrinking of world politics, of the new conceptions of the relationship between the domestic and international order, does not suggest that American policy-makers have arrived at a definitive answer to a perplexing question posed by contemporary internal conflicts: To what extent is it advisable for the United States to support decolonization and modernization at the risk of disorder inviting possible Communist take-overs? The controversial American actions in South Vietnam and the Dominican Republic underscore the continuing importance of the question and the continuing difficulty in establishing policy guidelines that may have validity for more than one case, for more than one geographical region.

Proxy wars, conflicts between foreign states fought on the soil of a third country using that country's resources and territory to achieve goals of external powers, are one form of violence in which conflicting American, Soviet, and Chinese interests may be expressed. The interests of less powerful states concerned with working out political differences in a regional setting also may be expressed in a proxy war, as have those of Egypt and Saudi Arabia in the Yemen civil war, a conflict supported by interested neighbors on national expansionist grounds. Richard Falk cites a wide range of interventions employed by third parties in internal disorders: unilateral interventions in which one nation intervenes in the internal affairs of another, as did the Soviet Union in Hungary or the United States under the Monroe Doctrine; counterintervention in which State A intervenes in State C to counter or offset interference of State B, along the lines of American interventions in Laos or Vietnam; regional interventions in which a group of states forms a juridical entity imposing a combined will on a dissenting member, as did the OAS with Cuba; and collective interventions under the aegis of the United Nations, as in the Congo.[14]

The Development of a United Nations Interest in Intrastate Conflict

Contemporary internal disorders, with social and economic aspects as well as political and military dimensions, with racial implications as well as ideological overtones, create special concerns for international organizations. The overriding interest of the United Nations in the maintenance of international peace and security has resulted in a growing involvement in the complexities of internal violence, an involvement the Australian delegate, Dr. Evatt, could not foresee in remarking to the Security Council on the Spanish question in 1946,

> When you look at the internal affairs of a country, you start off with the postulate that it is no business of any other nation to concern itself with how the people of that country govern themselves. That is, prima facie, primarily a matter of domestic concern, but if the facts indicate that the regime, by its nature, by its conduct, by its operations is likely to interfere with international peace and likely to be a menace to its neighbors, then the existence of that regime is no longer a matter of essentially domestic jurisdiction. The Charter is built on that basis.[15]

[14] Richard A. Falk, in Roland Stanger (ed.), *Essays on Intervention* (Columbus, Ohio: Ohio State University Press, 1964), pp. 40-41.

[15] Security Council, *Official Records*, First Year, First Series, No. 2, p. 352.

A threat to the peace occasioned by the outbreak of internal violence may arise from the behavior of local parties or from potential or actual external interventions. Internal disorders may appear to be "domestic" and will be characterized as such by parties who oppose U.N. involvement in particular cases. The concerns of the United Nations in internal disorders, apart from the often divergent national concerns of third-party states, are not confined to the maintenance or restoration of international peace and security. The interests of the Organization extend to a limitation of all violence, the promotion of political solutions and peaceful change, the protection of human rights, and the possible application of the principles of self-determination and legitimacy.

The conditions under which the United Nations expresses its concerns in cases of domestic strife and the means by which it responds to these disorders are determined by the interplay of national and international interests and influences. The international society embodied in the United Nations is a fluid one, composed of states who display different attitudes toward the United Nations and different capacities for using it as an instrument of national policy. The Organization is thus an arena in which governmental interests may be acted out and in which the interests of the larger international society may be advanced when competing national interests converge to permit a consensus. Since 1946 the United Nations has become an increasingly heterogeneous political institution, functioning as a "centre of intense, competitive, oblique diplomacy and equally intense open propaganda."[16] As a consequence

---

[16] Conor Cruise O'Brien, *Conflicting Concepts of the U.N.* (Leeds, England: Leeds University Press, 1964), p. 2.

of the nature of internal conflicts and of the Organization, the United Nations has moved pragmatically from situation to situation, eschewing rigid definitions or fixed roles committing individual members or groups of states to advance positions. The responses of the United Nations to internal violence, as distinct from the responses of individual members, are the expression of the views of many states, and therefore they may be slow in developing or may exhibit different tendencies at the same time. Policies of isolation aimed at restoring order may be accompanied by behind-the-scenes negotiations leading to active measures for conciliation. The individual disorders to be studied indicate the extent to which the United Nations fails to function as an autonomous agency superimposed on the environment.[17] Reflecting the political world, it is limited by that world in responding to internal conflicts as well as to international conflicts.

The United Nations is also limited by the circumstances of its founding and the drafting of its Charter. The Charter both expresses the concerns of the United Nations in internal disorders and sets limits to what the Organization is able to accomplish in realization of these objectives. The textual limits of the Charter may be of less importance in shaping the course of U.N. responses to internal conflicts than the political confines within which the Charter operates: for as Frederick Boland, President of the Fifteenth General Assembly, observed with reference to the Congo,

The U.N. is, of course, essentially not a judicial body. It doesn't proceed judicially, nor are legal considera-

[17] See Ernst B. Haas, "Dynamic Environment and Static System: Revolutionary Regimes in the United Nations," in Morton A. Kap-

tions, for the most part, uppermost in the minds of delegations. It is a political and diplomatic instrument, and like all political institutions, is operated very largely on the basis of expediency, covering itself always, of course, with the authorities provided for in its Charter. If there is no authority for an action, the action cannot be taken. But there are very able, gifted advisers of the United Nations who are usually able to find the necessary authorities.[18]

The framers of the U.N. Charter, like the authors of the Covenant of the League of Nations, were principally concerned with the problem of international war rather than intrastate violence. From the earliest Roosevelt-Churchill meetings through the subsequent international conferences devoted to peacetime planning, political leaders recorded convictions that provisions for the control of interstate violence must serve as the basis for postwar international organization. Internal disorders were not mentioned by name or category by the framers in the *travaux préparatoires* or in the finished Charter. In 1945 the threat of disruptive internal violence did not loom as large as the possible resumption of large-scale international war.[19] The Charter reflects

lan (ed.), *The Revolution in World Politics* (New York: John Wiley and Sons, 1962), p. 305.

[18] Quoted in Lyman M. Tondel, Jr. (ed.), *The Role of the United Nations in the Congo, Hammarskjöld Forums*, II, published for the Association of the Bar of the City of New York (Dobbs Ferry, New York: Oceana Press, 1963), p. 83.

[19] Thus, Article 1:1 states: "To maintain international peace and security, and to that end: to take effective collective measures for the prevention and removal of threats to the peace, and for the suppression of acts of aggression or other breaches of the peace, and to bring about by peaceful means, and in conformity with the principles of justice and international law, adjustment or settlement of interna-

the prevailing fears and preoccupations of its authors.

The incidence of internal disorders prior to World War II had resulted in the development of principles of neutrality, belligerency, and insurgency expressed in legal doctrines purporting to regulate state behavior in internal conflicts.[20] But the choices for third parties desiring to influence the outcome of civil strife were essentially political, in the absence of well-defined legal criteria. State practice before 1945 attests to the frequent deviations from the presumed norms of prewar legal doctrines.[21] The limits placed on permissible state action in internal conflicts were unclear. On paper, the finished Charter created an institution comparable in structure to the League and rooted in similar ideas of

---

tional disputes or situations which might lead to a breach of the peace."

[20] In generally accepted legal theory before 1945, the intervention of one state in the domestic affairs of another state or the premature recognition of a rebelling faction by a foreign power constituted a violation of international law. Two principal stages of internal hostilities—insurgency and belligerency—and the legal obligations arising from them were established in international law. Recognition of insurgency carried with it no legal rights or duties for third parties. A third party's acknowledgment of the fact of insurgency did not commit that state to undertake an obligation to aid either the insurgents or the legitimate government in a particular internal conflict. According to rule, the recognition of belligerency brought different legal relationships into play. Belligerency in law placed incumbents and insurgents on the same footing vis-à-vis third parties. As in interstate disputes, both belligerents in an internal conflict were entitled to exercise the rights of blockade against foreign states, who, in granting belligerency status to rebels and incumbents, undertook the obligations of neutrality toward both parties.

[21] The Monroe Doctrine, U.S. involvement in the affairs of the Caribbean and Central American republics, and the numerous national interventions in the Spanish Civil War are examples of state practice at variance with doctrine. For a detailed discussion, see Norman Padelford, *International Law and Diplomacy in the Spanish Civil Strife* (New York: Macmillan, 1939).

national sovereignty (Article 2:1),[22] domestic jurisdiction (Article 2:7),[23] and pacific settlement of disputes (Articles 2:3).[24] Departing from the Covenant, the

[22] Article 2:1 states: "The Organization is based on the principles of the sovereign equality of all its Members."

[23] Article 2:7 states: "Nothing contained in the present Charter shall authorize the United Nations to intervene in matters which are essentially within the domestic jurisdiction of any state or shall require the Members to submit such matters to settlement under the present Charter; but this principle shall not prejudice the application of enforcement measures under Chapter VII."

The inclusion of Article 2:7 in the Purposes and Principles of the Charter was originally intended to preclude the Organization from penetrating into the domestic life and social economy of the member states, although nothing in the Charter suggested that the United Nations had been granted such powers. The domestic jurisdiction principle did not exempt members from the application of enforcement measures under Chapter VII. In practice, the principle of domestic jurisdiction has been regarded as a political one subject to evolution rather than a legal one subject to international adjudication.

For thorough analysis of the framers' intentions, see Leland M. Goodrich and Edvard Hambro, *Charter of the United Nations: Commentary and Documents* (Boston: World Peace Foundation, 1949), rev. ed., pp. 110-121.

For general discussion of Article 2:7, see Quincy Wright, *International Law and the United Nations* (Delhi: Asia House, 1960), and *The Role of International Law in the Elimination of War* (Manchester: University of Manchester Press, 1961); Laurence Preuss, "Article 2:7 of the United Nations Charter and Matters of Domestic Jurisdiction," Hague *Recueil des Cours*, 1949; Sir Hersch Lauterpacht, *International Law and Human Rights* (New York: Praeger, 1950); and M. S. Rajan, *The United Nations and Domestic Jurisdiction* (New York: Asia Publishing House, 1961).

[24] Article 2:3 states: "All Members shall settle their international disputes by peaceful means in such a manner that international peace and security, and justice, are not endangered."

The Charter outlines suitable measures for disputants to employ in seeking non-violent solutions to conflicts. These measures include negotiation, enquiry, mediation, conciliation, arbitration, and judicial settlement (Article 33), plus resort to regional agencies or arrangements and "other peaceful means of their own choice." The Charter does not fail to provide techniques for adjustment of disputes or situations whose continuance is likely to endanger international peace and security (Articles 33, et al.) or to impair the general welfare or friendly relations among nations.

23

Charter incorporated additional commitments for members in the related fields of human rights, dependent peoples, and economic and social cooperation. As a treaty, the Charter purported to restrain signatories from the threat or use of force in their international relations (Article 2:4),[25] but the "outlawing" of force as an instrument of national policy was subject to the important exception contained in Article 51 respecting the "inherent right of individual or collective self-defense" in the event of "armed attack."[26] The framers of the Charter made no attempt to formulate rules for the legal relations of states in situations of subversion, revolution, or civil war.

The original signatories were equally concerned with the permissible uses of force in fulfillment of international obligations. The veto power (Article 27:3)[27] as-

[25] Article 2:4 states: "All Members shall refrain in their international relations from the threat or use of force against the territorial integrity or political independence of any state, or in any other manner inconsistent with the Purposes of the United Nations."

For a controversial treatment of the provisions of Article 2:4, see Julius Stone, *Aggression and World Order* (Berkeley: University of California Press, 1958), and *Legal Controls of International Conflict* (2nd ed.; London: Stevens, 1959).

[26] Article 51 states: "Nothing in the present Charter shall impair the inherent right of individual or collective self-defense if an armed attack occurs against a Member of the United Nations, until the Security Council has taken measures necessary to maintain international peace and security. Measures taken by Members in the exercise of this right of self-defense shall be immediately reported to the Security Council and shall not in any way affect the authority and responsibility of the Security Council under the present Charter to take at any time such action as it deems necessary in order to maintain or restore international peace and security."

[27] Article 27:3 states: "Decisions of the Security Council on all other matters shall be made by an affirmative vote of seven members including the concurring votes of the permanent members; provided that, in decisions under Chapter VI, and under paragraph 3 of Article 52, a party to a dispute shall abstain from voting."

sured members that the United Nations would not undertake collective enforcement measures against the permanent members of the Security Council. Nor would the Council undertake to apply sanctions if the permanent members disagreed on the object of enforcement. The Charter's security system, elaborated in a series of graduated steps (Articles 39-49), was predicated on the assumption that members would supply the Organization with sufficient military resources for its enforcement needs (Article 43).[28] These resources would be employed in cases of aggression when the major powers agreed to sponsor concerted action against less powerful states. The Security Council's primary responsibility for maintaining international peace and security (Article 24)[29] would be exercised in serious dis-

[28] Article 43 states:

"1. All Members of the United Nations, in order to contribute to the maintenance of international peace and security, undertake to make available to the Security Council, on its call and in accordance with a special agreement or agreements, armed forces, assistance, and facilities, including rights of passage, necessary for the purpose of maintaining international peace and security.

"2. Such agreement or agreements shall govern the numbers and types of forces, their degree of readiness and general location, and the nature of the facilities and assistance to be provided.

"3. The agreement or agreements shall be negotiated as soon as possible on the initiative of the Security Council. They shall be concluded between the Security Council and Members or between the Security Council and groups of Members and shall be subject to ratification by the signatory states in accordance with their respective constitutional processes."

[29] Article 24 states in part:

"1. In order to ensure prompt and effective action by the United Nations, its Members confer on the Security Council primary responsibility for the maintenance of international peace and security, and agree that in carrying out its duties under this responsibility the Security Council acts on their behalf.

"2. In discharging these duties the Security Council shall act in accordance with the Purposes and Principles of the United Nations.

putes whose continuance challenged world order. The Assembly's broad powers of discussion and recommendation (Articles 10 and 14)[30] would embrace less threatening situations, the framers assumed.

In joining the United Nations, the colonial powers were anxious to safeguard their territorial interests. Yet in accepting the principles enshrined in Articles 55, 56, 73, and 76,[31] they appeared to acknowledge that the

---

The specific powers granted to the Security Council for the discharge of these duties are laid down in Chapters VI, VII, VIII, and XII."

[30] Article 10 states: "The General Assembly may discuss any questions or any matters within the scope of the present Charter or relating to the powers and functions of any organs provided for in the present Charter, and, except as provided in Article 12, may make recommendations to the Members of the United Nations or to the Security Council or to both on any such questions or matters."

Article 14 states: "Subject to the provisions of Article 12, the General Assembly may recommend measures for the peaceful adjustment of any situation, regardless of origin, which it deems likely to impair the general welfare or friendly relations among nations, including situations resulting from a violation of the provisions of the present Charter setting forth the Purposes and Principles of the United Nations."

[31] Article 55 states: "With a view to the creation of conditions of stability and well-being which are necessary for peaceful and friendly relations among nations based on respect for the principle of equal rights and self-determination of peoples, the United Nations shall promote:

a. higher standards of living, full employment, and conditions of economic and social progress and development;

b. solutions of international economic, social, health, and related problems; and international cultural and educational co-operation; and

c. universal respect for, and observance of, human rights and fundamental freedoms for all without distinction as to race, sex, language, or religion."

Article 56 states: "All Members pledge themselves to take joint and separate action in cooperation with the Organization for the achievement of the purposes set forth in Article 55."

Article 73 states, in part: "Members of the United Nations which have or assume responsibilities for the administration of territories whose peoples have not yet attained a full measure of self-govern-

Charter's human rights provisions placed some limitations on a government's power to coerce its citizenry. The Security Council's authorization to "investigate any dispute, or any situation which might lead to interna-

---

ment recognize the principle that the interests of the inhabitants of these territories are paramount, and accept as a sacred trust the obligation to promote to the utmost, within the system of international peace and security established by the present Charter, the well-being of the inhabitants of these territories, and, to this end:

a. to ensure, with due respect for the culture of the peoples concerned, their political, economic, social, and educational advancement, their just treatment, and their protection against abuses;

b. to develop self-government, and to take due account of the political aspirations of the peoples, and to assist them in the progressive development of their free political institutions, according to the particular circumstances of each territory and its peoples and their varying stages of advancement;

c. to further international peace and security;

d. to promote constructive measures of development, to encourage research, and to cooperate with one another and, when and where appropriate, with specialized international bodies with a view to the practical achievement of the social, economic, and scientific purposes set forth in this Article."

Article 76 states: "The basic objectives of the trusteeship system, in accordance with the Purposes of the United Nations laid down in Article 1 of the present Charter, shall be:

a. to further international peace and security;

b. to promote the political, economic, social, and educational advancement of the inhabitants of the trust territories, and their progressive development towards self-government or independence as may be appropriate to the particular circumstances of each territory and its peoples and the freely expressed wishes of the peoples concerned, and as may be provided by the terms of each trusteeship agreement;

c. to encourage respect for human rights and for fundamental freedoms for all without distinction as to race, sex, language, or religion, and to encourage recognition of the interdependence of the peoples of the world; and

d. to ensure equal treatment in social, economic, and commercial matters for all Members of the United Nations and their nationals, and also equal treatment for the latter in the administration of justice, without prejudice to the attainment of the foregoing objectives and subject to the provisions of Article 80."

tional friction" (Article 34)[32] and to "determine the existence of any threat to the peace, breach of the peace, or act of aggression" and make recommendations (Article 39)[33] suggested that the Organization *might* deal with civil war situations if they endangered international stability. In sum, "the Charter concentrates on the problem of international war, ignoring the issues of civil war except in cases where domestic strife appears likely to develop significant international ramifications. The Charter's concern with international war is absolute, its concern with war within states is conditional."[34]

Many of the framers' assumptions were challenged by events in the immediate postwar political world in which the new international organization would function. The rapid breakdown of the wartime alliance and the accelerating arms race doomed attempts to activate Article 43. The fruitless negotiations over the size, composition, powers, and duties of the proposed force revealed the extent of Soviet-American discord within the Organization and outside its councils. Deprived of its cornerstone, the U.N. enforcement system remained a theoretical construction as nations entrusted their defense to military coalitions of like-minded allies.

[32] Article 34 states: "The Security Council may investigate any dispute, or any situation which might lead to international friction or give rise to a dispute, in order to determine whether the continuance of the dispute or situation is likely to endanger the maintenance of international peace and security."

[33] Article 39 states: "The Security Council shall determine the existence of any threat to the peace, breach of the peace, or act of aggression and shall make recommendations, or decide what measures shall be taken in accordance with Articles 41 and 42, to maintain or restore international peace and security."

[34] Inis Claude, "The United Nations and the Use of Force," *International Conciliation*, No. 532 (March 1961), p. 326.

Throughout the United Nations' two decades, questions of internal order, chiefly residual problems stemming from the aftermath of war and the termination of colonialism, have crowded the agendas of the Assembly and Council. The Charter has served as the legal basis for the Organization's exercise of some form of control over internal violence threatening peace. The flexibility of the United Nations' constitutional document has enabled the enlarged membership to cope with types of violence the Charter's framers failed to mention in specific terms. The Security Council, in its handling of a series of internal disorders, has adopted an increasingly broad interpretation of its responsibilities for the maintenance of international peace and security. The steadily enlarging membership has favored the view of the British representative who, in pressing for U.N. consideration of the Korean violence in 1950, argued that

a civil war in certain circumstances might well, under Article 39 of the Charter, constitute a "threat to the peace" or even a "breach of the peace," and if the Security Council so decided, there would be nothing whatever to prevent its taking any action it liked in order to put an end to the incident, even if it should involve two or more portions of the same international entity.[35]

The Assembly, with its broad powers of discussion and recommendation, has also played a role in the United Nations' consideration of internal conflicts, including those in Indonesia, Algeria, and Angola. The 1950 Uniting for Peace Resolution[36] facilitated Assembly

[35] Security Council, *Official Records*, Fifth Year, No. 28, 486th Meeting (August 11, 1950), p. 6.
[36] General Assembly Resolution 377 (V), November 3, 1950.

consideration of violence in Hungary, the Congo, and Lebanon when the Council's deadlock prevented further action. The Assembly has augmented the legal basis for international control of internal conflicts by means of general resolutions on civil strife. States have often cited these resolutions in preference to Charter articles when urging U.N. action in specific internal disputes. Prior to the doubling of the Organization's membership, the Assembly passed two resolutions embodying statements of principle bearing on the conduct of third parties in internal conflicts. The 1949 Essentials of Peace Resolution called upon nations to "refrain from any threats or acts, direct or indirect, aimed at impairing the freedom, independence or integrity of any state, at fomenting civil strife and subverting the will of the people in any state."[37] The 1950 Peace Through Deeds Resolution condemned outside intervention in a state's internal affairs aimed at altering the legitimate government by threat or use of force and affirmed that "whatever the weapon used, any aggression whether committed openly or by fomenting civil strife in the interest of a foreign power or otherwise is the gravest of crimes against peace."[38] Recourse to these principles may be traced in Council and Assembly resolutions adopted during the United Nations' consideration of violence in Greece, Lebanon, Laos, and the Congo. Significantly, neither the Essentials of Peace nor the Peace Through Deeds Resolutions mentions international law as the standard for ascertaining acceptable state conduct. State behavior, while not equivalent to international law, nevertheless is an index of adherence to it, and prevailing practice attests to the

[37] General Assembly Resolution 290 (IV), December 1, 1949.
[38] General Assembly Resolutions 380 and 381 (V), November 17, 1950.

frequent deviations from the non-intervention norms of these resolutions.

It would be difficult to furnish evidence that states consider themselves bound by these resolutions, that states have accepted either of these resolutions as constituting new legal obligations for themselves, as constituting "community-authorized norms"[39] precluding national interventions. As statements of principle endorsed by the United Nations, the resolutions suggest suitable or desirable norms of conduct for participants in contemporary world politics.[40] But while the Charter advances beyond the League Covenant in establishing some restraints on national uses of force (Article 2:4), effective control of force remains on the national level and governs the expectations and behavior of all participants in world politics.[41]

It is also clear that the standards of customary international law pertaining to intervention have become outworn as interventions have increased. As a result, scholarly attempts to ascertain what international law

[39] See Richard A. Falk, in Stanger, pp. 40-44.

[40] Similar norms of conduct are set forth in the recent General Assembly declaration on the inadmissibility of intervention in the domestic affairs of other states and the protection of their independence and sovereignty. The declaration [General Assembly Resolution 2131 (XX), December 21, 1965], recommended by the First Committee, was adopted by a vote of 109 to 1, with one abstention (Britain). Reaffirming the principle of non-intervention advanced in the charters of the OAS, OAU and the League of Arab States, the resolution states that "no States shall organize, assist, foment, finance, incite or tolerate subversive, terrorist or armed activities directed to the violent overthrow of the regime of another State, or interfere in the civil strife of another State" (para. 2). The resolution was introduced by 57 states, including a large number of African and Latin American countries who have special interests in the conduct of third parties in view of the frequency of civil strife in their own regions.

[41] Richard A. Falk, *Law, Morality and War in the Contemporary World* (New York: Praeger, 1963), p. 39.

"permits" have produced disagreement. Quincy Wright argues that

> International law does not permit the use of force in the territory of another state on invitation either of the recognized or the insurgent government in times of rebellion, insurrection or civil war. Since international law recognizes the right of revolution it cannot permit other states to intervene to prevent it. The United Nations itself cannot intervene in civil strife unless it concludes that such strife threatens international peace and security or violates an internationally recognized cease-fire line.[42]

For other scholars, Wright's statement of what international law "permits" does not provide a suitable measure for judging postwar state practice in internal conflicts.[43] Louis Henkin, asserting that the fundamental law of the Charter, the prohibition on unilateral force

[42] Quincy Wright, quoted in Benjamin Cohen, *The United Nations: Constitutional Development, Growth and Possibilities* (Cambridge: Harvard University Press, 1961), p. 54. On the basis of this reasoning, Wright concludes that an administering authority's police action in a local uprising, for example, the British reaction to the turmoil in Borneo in 1963 would be "legal," that is, a matter of domestic concern. But with reference to these same standards Wright asserts that the U.S. intervention in Lebanon in 1958 was "illegal" because: (a) it occurred when the outcome of the conflict was not certain, hence, neither faction should have received aid; (b) it could not be justified in terms of self-defense; (c) it occurred in response to an improper invitation of the Chamoun government tendered before the nature of the revolt and the extent of indirect aggression could be ascertained. Quincy Wright, "United States Intervention in the Lebanon," *American Journal of International Law*, LIII (January 1959), 112ff.

[43] As Richard Falk argues, "this way of perceiving traditional international law suffers from its tendency to repress a recognition of the possible contradictions between rigid adherence to ideals of self-determination, self-defense, domestic jurisdiction, nonintervention, and the maintenance of peace." Richard A. Falk, "Janus Tormented: The International Law of Internal War," in Rosenau, pp. 228-229.

in international relations, remains valid despite the cold war, the advent of nuclear weapons, and the admission of new states to the United Nations, suggests that in the absence of Charter provisions barring particular kinds of interventions, the right "to intervene" by recognizing insurgency and belligerency or asserting neutrality in a civil war may be as uncertain today as in the nineteenth century. Thus a U.N. "political role" aimed at maintaining the independence of a country experiencing conflict by excluding foreign intervention may yield greater rewards than efforts to formulate "rules" governing such intervention.[44]

Henkin's emphasis on the United Nations' political role in internal disorders accords with the late Secretary-General Hammarskjöld's conviction that the Organization's value in these conflicts depends upon its ability to keep newly arising conflicts outside the arena of superpower competition:

> Agreement may be achieved because of a mutual interest among the Big Powers to avoid having a regional or local conflict drawn into the sphere of bloc politics . . . both blocs have an interest in avoiding such an extension of the area of conflict because of the threatening consequences were the localization of conflict to fail. . . .[45]

But what may appear to be "agreement" among the major powers to avoid having a regional or local conflict drawn into the sphere of bloc politics may be little

[44] Louis Henkin, "Force, Intervention and Neutrality in International Law," American Society of International Law, *Proceedings*, 1963, p. 147.

[45] Introduction to the Annual Report of the Secretary-General, 1959-1960. General Assembly, *Official Records*, Fifteenth Session, Supplement No. 1A (A/4390 Add. 1), pp. 4-5.

more than a temporary consensus while each "bloc leader" formulates national policy positions which may or may not involve support for U.N. participation. In some instances the Organization may serve as a channel through which larger states may bring their strength to bear without seeming to do so, through which they may participate in securing desired outcomes without risking war or appearing to intervene unilaterally.

Significantly, the development of a U.N. interest in internal disorders is apparent apart from the infrequent convergence of interests of the superpowers. Responsible for this interest, and for the values of international peace and self-determination the Organization is now committed to foster, are a group of "middle powers" (middle in terms of size and political influence) and newer members. In the Assembly or as non-permanent members of the Security Council, the middle and smaller powers are an important source of conciliation between major powers at odds over specific facets of U.N. involvement in particular internal conflicts. The individual cases to be examined find delegates of the Scandinavian countries, Ireland, Australia, and certain Latin American countries playing instrumental parts in drafting and sponsoring compromise resolutions, in private negotiations, and in providing field personnel when needed. For these states, the United Nations is a diplomatic field in which they may exercise some control over events of prime concern to the superpowers. For the modernizing member-states, whose societies are vulnerable to internal strife and external interventions, the United Nations is a possible source of protection and a forum in which their influence may shape the course of internal violence in post-colonial and other developing countries.

Conclusion

The preceding analysis has stressed that the bases of international concern in contemporary internal disorders are related to the status of these conflicts in world politics. Given the diminishing relevance of national boundaries to economic activity, military strategy, and ideological commitment in the present international system, the line between internal and international conflict has become increasingly difficult to draw. Struggles for internal supremacy are seen by participants at home and abroad as part of larger conflicts of a racial, anti-colonialist, or cold-war character involving the risk of escalation and thereby constituting potential or actual threats to international peace and security. Contemporary internal violence stimulates international concerns in world order, peaceful change, and human rights, in goals difficult to attain in the volatile circumstances of conflicts prone to various kinds of interventions by competing third parties who may seek to maximize narrower national interests. The ways in which tensions between national and international concerns affect the United Nations' capacity to assist in limiting intrastate violence and promoting political solutions to several types of internal disorder are explored in Chapters 2, 3, and 4.

CHAPTER II

The United Nations Role in Colonial Wars

THE transition of territories from colonialism to independence, a transition effected since the end of World War II, has destabilized the international system. The old relationships evolved between colonial administrations and their colonies have been shattered, and newer connections between the "emerging" nations and older sovereign entities are lacking in order or permanence. The process of decolonization has posed the general problem of peaceful change in a challenging form. It has not been a "peaceful" process for the groups and political entities involved directly; it has been "peaceful" only in terms of the avoidance of large-scale interstate violence growing out of tensions engendered by the transition. Increasingly since 1946, non-governments have used violence within territories in order to effect a termination of foreign rule. Insurrectionary violence in colonial areas has raised acute problems for the United Nations. For, as Rupert Emerson points out, international law and international organization are more suited to the maintenance of an established status quo: "attractive as is the conception of peaceful change, it has not been possible to clothe it in acceptable institutional forms."[1] Moreover, he observes, "independence, in prospect or achieved, cannot be counted upon to weld disparate peoples into national homogeneity and may in fact aggravate rather than allay discord."[2]

The protracted struggles of local groups for inde-

[1] Rupert Emerson, *From Empire to Nation* (Cambridge: Harvard University Press, 1960), p. 393.
[2] *Ibid.*, p. 342.

pendence, first in Indonesia, then, in Algeria, and finally in Angola, have involved the United Nations in asymmetrical conflicts in which incumbents have enjoyed a greater preponderance of power at the initial stages of disorder. The Indonesian, Algerian, and Angolan conflicts are examples of revolutionary wars taking place in territories in which the government is distant geographically, socially, and politically from the indigenous population. Unlike reformist coups undertaken by groups already participating in the political system of a state, revolutionary wars are conducted by groups outside the administrative power structure. The Dutch, the French, and the Portuguese have confronted nongovernmental cliques, parties or movements possessing a qualitatively different type of political organization. Incumbent regimes have sought to quell rebellious factions and to restore or maintain their own authority as legitimate, recognized governments. Insurgents have sought to end foreign domination and to establish governmental structures under local control.

Incumbent regimes have been forced to make consequential decisions in meeting violence in their colonial territories. They have had to decide whether to regard uprisings as a sign of temporary unrest or as a total challenge to law and order, a challenge possibly backed by outside parties. Incumbents have had to decide whether to commit all their resources or few to the deterrence or containment of disorder. They have had to consider the extent to which a continuation of conflict would permit rebel groups to develop their own outside contacts, to acquire an international personality and provisional membership in the international system.[3] The

[3] Modelski, pp. 4ff.

Dutch, French, and Portuguese governments, weighing the threats posed by insurgent groups in Indonesia, Algeria, and Angola, have sought to isolate these conflicts from outside intrusion in hopes that internal concessions short of abdication would suffice to end disorder. Each European government, in its turn, opposed the formal internationalization of the conflict, fearing that the United Nations might confer undue status on the rebelling faction and expose shortcomings of its administration.

The insurgents in Indonesia, Algeria, and Angola favored U.N. involvement for the same reasons the European states opposed a role for the Organization: first, as a means of publicizing grievances against repressive regimes, thereby enlisting broader sympathy for rebel goals; and second, as a means of enhancing bargaining positions and compensating for military weaknesses. In the course of the United Nations' involvement in the three colonial wars, third-party states have played influential roles in urging the Council and Assembly to regard the disorders as threats to the peace or breaches of the peace. Australia played such a role in the Indonesian case; the newer members of the Organization, especially the Black African states, played similar roles in the Algerian and Angolan cases. In all three colonial wars the Organization's efforts to confine hostilities, to restore order, to foster self-determination, and to encourage viable political settlements have been hampered by the reluctance of incumbents and insurgents to legitimize each other, to accord the recognition implied in acceding to negotiations. The initial disparity in power between opponents in colonial wars, between administering powers seated in the Organization and rebellious factions without formal representation, has not precluded U.N. political organs from expressing definite preferences for change favorable to insurgents.

Although the present majority's overwhelming preoccupation with colonialism in all its facets has created an atmosphere for the discussion of the Angolan question which contrasts with that obtaining when the Organization coped with the Indonesian question in the late 1940's, certain general similarities in the character of colonial wars and the United Nations' role in them emerge from a detailed consideration of the United Nations' response to three conflicts brought to its attention at different periods of its history. The effect of shifting attitudes and approaches, some involving permanent members of the Security Council, others involving incumbent regimes or newer members, also must be weighed in assessing the Organization's role in colonial wars.

Indonesia

The United Nations' involvement in Indonesia when internal strife erupted there in 1947 was complicated by the attitude of the Dutch government, which regarded its uses of force as a legitimate exercise of police powers, and by the attitude of the insurgents, who regarded their uses of force as an integral part of the "right of revolution." But because the Indonesian insurgents were militarily weak, they had much to gain by a cessation of hostilities and U.N. resolutions looking toward a political settlement. The United Nations' pro-Western majority sought to assuage the Netherlands while yielding to local desires for independence. The Netherlands government, intent on retaining influence if not control in Indonesia, took a restrictive approach to U.N. consideration of the dispute. Britain and France, the leading colonial powers when the conflict came to the Organization's attention, favored a settlement outside the United Nations and vigorously opposed sending an investigatory or supervisory body to the scene.

The Indonesian question required the membership to consider the applicability of Articles 2:7, 2:4, 39, 34, and 35. A colonial problem with roots in the Japanese occupation, the Indonesian conflict presented the Council with delicate questions of competence. The Australian draft resolution referred to a "breach of the peace" (Article 39) and an existing state of warfare between two states. The Netherlands government contended that Indonesia was a matter essentially within its domestic jurisdiction and that Dutch military action was a domestic police activity permissible under Article 2:4, without consequence for international peace and security. The Linggadjati agreement of March 25, 1947, negotiated by the parties themselves, provided for de facto recognition of an Indonesian Republic in Java, Madura, and Sumatra linked to the Netherlands in a union. This solution had represented concessions on both sides. The Dutch government, regarding Japanese occupation of Indonesia as a hiatus in its rule, pressed for federal states in the new union, while the Indonesian Republican forces wanted de jure recognition as well as de facto control. The Dutch denied that in concluding the Linggadjati agreement the Netherlands had conferred recognition as a sovereign state on the Republic regime.

When the Indonesian question came before the Security Council in the summer of 1947, member-states lacked detailed knowledge of the fighting between the colonial power and the insurgent forces. The Council heard statements from the Soviet delegate urging that the troops of both sides withdraw to antebellum positions,[4] and from the U.S. representative stressing the hazards of withdrawal of the civil administration from its positions.[5] The Council's first resolution, framed in general terms, called for the cessation of hostilities, arbitration, and a good offices committee to assist in the pacific settlement of the dispute.[6]

Procedures were employed in the Council's consideration of the Indonesian case that had ramifications for later controversies. At American behest, references to specific Charter articles were deleted from the first and subsequent draft resolutions. Issues of competence were sidestepped as the Council, in its resolution of August 1, 1947, "called upon" parties to "cease hostilities forthwith" in the language of Article 40,[7] without benefit of a formal finding under Article 39. The Council had made no prior determination of its competence to intervene nor of the rebelling faction's legal status.[8]

[4] Security Council, *Official Records*, Second Year, No. 68, 172nd Meeting (August 1, 1947), p. 1665.

[5] *Ibid.*, p. 1704.

[6] Security Council Resolution S/525, August 1, 1947.

[7] Article 40 states: "In order to prevent an aggravation of the situation, the Security Council may, before making the recommendations or deciding upon the measures provided for in Article 39, call upon the parties concerned to comply with such provisional measures as it deems necessary or desirable. Such provisional measures shall be without prejudice to the rights, claims, or position of the parties concerned. The Security Council shall duly take account of failure to comply with such provisional measures."

[8] Later the Council named the rebels a party to U.N. good offices and invited its representatives to participate in Council sessions without explicitly ruling on its qualifications under Article 32.

Article 32 states: "Any Member of the United Nations which is not a member of the Security Council or any state which is not a Member of the United Nations, if it is a party to a dispute under consideration by the Security Council, shall be invited to participate,

41

In responding to the demands of the immediate situation in which peace appeared to be threatened, the Council did not offer clear guidelines as to the interpretation of Article 2:7 it favored:

> The question of jurisdiction was never explicitly decided by the Council, though the action subsequently taken could only have been justified on the assumption that competence to act existed. Nor was it made clear whether the action of the Council was based on the exception to the domestic jurisdiction principle or on the view that the matter was not essentially within the domestic jurisdiction of the Netherlands.[9]

Subsequent to the Council's resolution of August 1st, the Dutch military forces made territorial advances. In renewed Council debate, the Brazilian delegate warned of the dangers of a withdrawal of forces, suggesting that disorder might ensue causing "new protests and complaints and, perhaps, new violence."[10] The Brazilian representative based his views on the fact that a neutral military body capable of supervising withdrawal was not present on the scene. The Council's resolution of November 1, 1947, informed the parties that the earlier August resolution should not be interpreted as allowing either the Dutch or the Indonesians to seize territory not held on August 4th.[11] The No-

---

without vote, in the discussion relating to the dispute. The Security Council shall lay down such conditions as it deems just for the participation of a state which is not a Member of the United Nations."

[9] Goodrich and Hambro, p. 118.

[10] Security Council, *Official Records*, Second Year, No. 96, 210th Meeting (October 11, 1947), p. 2548.

[11] Security Council Resolution S/597, November 1, 1947.

vember resolution did not establish a new subsidiary organ with the specific assignment of supervising the parties' compliance with the Council's recommendations. Instead, the parties were invited to confer with each other directly or via the Good Offices Committee.

The Good Offices Committee, composed of Belgium as the Netherlands choice, Australia as the Indonesian choice, and the United States, was not constituted as a board of arbitration or even mediation. Either party or the Council could veto its recommendations. Despite its vague mandate, the Committee did not confine its work to technical aspects of good offices but undertook to advance substantive proposals. As the middleman in the Security Council, the United States sought to hold the question of the Council's competence in abeyance while peaceful settlement methods were tried. As the middleman on the Good Offices Committee, the United States lent its support to a truce agreement of January 17, 1948, establishing demilitarized zones and calling for withdrawal of forces. In addition, the parties accepted as a basis for discussion twelve (later eighteen) principles providing for the transfer of sovereignty, convening of a constitutional convention, and Indonesian independence.[12] But the unequal power relations of the disputants led to a breakdown of these arrangements (known collectively as the Renville Agreement) in the months following May 1948. Heightened tension and economic unrest, observed by the Committee in an interim report to the Council, resulted in the launching of the second Netherlands police action in December 1948. Clearly, resumed hostilities indicated a failure of

[12] Alastair Taylor, *Indonesian Independence and the United Nations* (Ithaca: Cornell University Press, 1960), pp. 96-97.

the Council's good offices, founded on a "piecemeal approach" separating the political and military aspects of the controversy.[13] A series of draft resolutions introduced in debate called for condemnation of Dutch "aggression" and a new commission composed of representatives of the entire Council to oversee a political settlement (U.S.S.R.); cessation of hostilities and additional reports of the Good Offices Committee (U.S.). The Council, rejecting the Netherlands reading of Articles 2:7 and 39, and other arguments against its competence, passed a resolution calling for a cease-fire. The Council's resolutions on the Indonesian question prior to January 1949 had failed to mention specific Charter articles as the basis for U.N. competence, nor did they contain judgments as to the status of the two parties to the colonial war. The resolution of January 28, 1949, contained far-reaching political provisions. It called for the establishment of a United States of Indonesia, release of all political prisoners, return of the Republican administration to Jakarta, and restoration of its territory. The resolution also called for the transfer of sovereignty to Indonesia after free elections and for the formation of a United Nations Commission on Indonesia to act as the Council's representative and to report on implementation.[14] The resolution expressed the concurrence of other Council members with the American view that insistence on withdrawal of Netherlands forces in the resolution might neglect local problems attending withdrawal procedures.[15] But the Council's resolution made the initiation of political discussions

[13] See *ibid.*, pp. 365-373.

[14] Security Council Resolution S/1234, January 28, 1949.

[15] Security Council, *Official Records*, Fourth Year, No. 6, 402nd Meeting (January 21, 1949), p. 8.

conditional on the restoration of order and the creation of conditions allowing the Indonesian Republic freedom of participation in negotiations.

Political accord between the major powers in the Council made agreement possible on the use of the United Nations Commission for Indonesia as an instrument for parties to consult in working out concrete arrangements for the cessation of hostilities and a return to law and order in conformity with the Council's resolution. When both sides had more to gain by cooperating with negotiations than by sabotaging them, UNCI was helpful in instigating procedures and mediating differences. It helped to restore the civilian government in Jakarta and brought the Federalists into consultation on the structure of the interim government. After the transfer of sovereignty, UNCI lapsed back into a good-offices role, consulted infrequently, as needed by the parties.

A final solution to the Indonesian internal war developed out of a bilateral framework. The Netherlands government failed to implement relevant parts of the January 28th resolution, calling instead for a round-table conference with both the Republicans and the Federalists. The Security Council, after urging compliance with the resolution, approved the Hague talks, which led to eventual settlement. The Organization's interest in the Indonesian question did help to modify the intransigent positions of interested parties and to secure Indonesia's independence and admission to the United Nations as a sovereign state. Nevertheless, the pressures brought to bear by the United States on the Netherlands, such as the cancellation of Marshall Plan aid to the Dutch in Indonesia, were of great consequence in changing Dutch policies.[16] Although the Council's approach to the Indonesian question revealed an unfamiliarity with Asian problems and although its collective decisions were often a priori expediencies with political rather than juridical or economic factors preeminent, the success of the Organization in helping to achieve a solution to the Indonesian conflict is acknowledged by most observers.

Many of the reasons for the United Nations' effectiveness in containing local violence in the Indonesian colonial war are to be found in the political circumstances of the period in which the conflict came to the Organization. The decolonization process was beginning in 1947. The direct interests of the Soviet Union and the United States which were to characterize later internal conflicts in Asia had not emerged when violence broke out in Indonesia. The Council was able to exercise its primary responsibilities for the maintenance of international peace and security because the two superpowers had no interest in prolonging the conflict, nor did they attempt to turn the disorder into a proxy war. The Soviet Union urged all states to reject Dutch claims of domestic jurisdiction, but was reluctant to support the Republicans wholeheartedly because the Sukarno-Hatta leadership had crushed a Communist uprising in Indonesia in 1948. The Russians therefore went along with suggestions for a U.N. commission as a possible method for terminating a disorder they had no immediate interest in continuing. The United States used its influence bilaterally as well as in the United Nations to urge

[16] See J. Foster Collins, "The United Nations and Indonesia," *International Conciliation*, No. 458 (March 1950), pp. 176-183.

Dutch compliance with Council resolutions looking toward political settlement after hostilities.

The U.N. involvement in the Indonesian conflict occurred in the period of Western dominance in the Organization, before the influx of newer states into the Assembly, before the era of peace-keeping operations. The subsidiary organs established by the Council in the Indonesian case placed no financial burdens on the Organization and created no dissension in the Council. But the difficulties the Good Offices Committee experienced in seeking to attain and monitor a lasting cease-fire agreement in order to implement Council resolutions calling for the end of hostilities[17] indicated that local parties to the disorder could easily jeopardize a Council agreement on suitable courses of action for the United Nations and disputants to take in halting internal violence. These difficulties were to reappear, although in somewhat different form, in the United Nations' involvement in later internal conflicts, notably the Congo and Cyprus disorders.

Algeria

By 1955 the decolonization process had accelerated in pace. In January of that year, Saudi Arabia brought to the attention of the Security Council the "grave situation in Algeria." In July 1955, fourteen African and Asian states asked that the Algerian question be placed on the agenda of the tenth General Assembly. The French government was intent upon preventing U.N.

---

[17] The military observers of the U.N.'s Good Offices Committee encountered difficulties in monitoring activities in the field due to actions of the Dutch officials in Indonesia. Moreover, the fact that the Republican government had stopped functioning meant that there were no competent authorities to implement the Council's cease-fire resolution. See Taylor, pp. 365ff.

consideration of the colonial war and buttressed its position with the argument that as Algeria was an integral part of France, U.N. discussion or action would constitute a violation of Article 2:7. After a lengthy debate in which the United States and Britain supported the French position, the General Committee recommended that the Assembly exclude the Algerian question from its agenda. But the combined votes of the Afro-Asian group, some Latin American states, and the Soviet Union formed a majority large enough to overrule the General Committee's recommendation. The French government's representatives refused to take part in any meetings of the Assembly or its committees. France returned to the Assembly after the First Committee adopted a procedural motion, submitted by India, which recommended that the Assembly give no further attention to the Algerian item at the tenth session. At the eleventh Assembly, the Algerian question was debated, but a mild resolution was passed, a resolution expressing the hope that "a spirit of co-operation, a peaceful, democratic and just solution will be found."[18]

The Afro-Asian demands for a stronger U.N. resolution were evident in the meetings of the twelfth Assembly. A compromise resolution was adopted that took note of the offer of the good offices of Moroccan and Tunisian leaders and expressed the wish that "*pourparlers* will be entered into, and other appropriate means utilized."[19] De Gaulle's return to power in May 1958 appeared to promise the beginning of a fruitful era in Algerian-French relations. Although the General's promise of "a preferred place" for Algeria was

---

[18] General Assembly Resolution 1012 (XI), February 15, 1957.
[19] General Assembly Resolution 1184 (XII), December 10, 1957.

vague, it calmed some of the fears of the European settlers who advocated a strong stand against the Front of
National Liberation (FLN). The FLN vowed to continue its fight for Algerian independence, and announced the formation of a Provisional Government
of the Algerian Republic (GPRA).

At the thirteenth Assembly, seventeen African and
Asian states sponsored a resolution terming the "war"
in Algeria a threat to international peace and security,
and calling for "negotiations between the two parties
concerned." The resolution, which failed of adoption in
a modified form, recognized the "right of the Algerian
people to independence."[20] France did not participate
in the 1958 debates or in the 1959 deliberations. In a
key address in September 1959, De Gaulle pledged that
all Algerians would be asked to choose one of three
alternatives for the future: (1) independence; (2) "out-
and-out identification with France"; and (3) "government of Algerians by Algerians, backed up by French
help and in close relationship with her," under a federal regime.[21] A referendum was promised for four years
after the attainment of peace (defined as a state of affairs in which fewer than 200 people per year died as
a result of hostilities), and safe conduct was assured to
nationalist leaders who wished to settle the matter of
a military cease-fire.

The FLN or GPRA declared its readiness to negotiate
with the French leader, but, hopeful of independence
without partition, the GPRA insisted that political as
well as military aspects of the cease-fire be discussed.

[20] U.N. Doc. A/4075, December 13, 1958.
[21] *French Affairs*, No. 90, September 16, 1959, New York, French
Embassy Press and Information Service.

49

When the fourteenth Assembly opened, many Asian and African delegates stated that they believed the Assembly could "render a useful service by attempting to clarify the issues (and helping) to bring the two parties together."[22] The French government again refused to take part in debates, and many representatives were reluctant to advance even an innocuous resolution on grounds that the prospects for settlement might be impaired. Therefore a mild resolution failed to gain the necessary votes in the Assembly.

In 1960, sixteen new African states and Cyprus joined the Afro-Asian group in sponsoring a resolution calling for a referendum under U.N. auspices, but a split in the group resulted in the failure of the Assembly to pass this draft resolution. The Brazzaville group (including the former French territories except Mali) led those states in favor of a moderate U.N. stand to vote for the adoption of the first resolution passed on the Algerian question since 1957. The Organization's role in "contributing" to "effective guarantees to ensure . . . self-determination" was left vague in a resolution calling for "respect for the unity and territorial integrity of Algeria."[23]

The GPRA continued to strengthen its international position during 1960-61, taking part in meetings of the Casablanca powers (U.A.R., Ghana, Guinea, Mali, and Morocco) and securing recognition (de jure or de facto) from twenty-seven countries.[24] In January 1961, De Gaulle received support for his policy of self-determi-

[22] General Assembly, *Official Records*, Fourteenth Session, First Committee, 1070th Meeting (December 2, 1959), para. 1.
[23] General Assembly Resolution 1573 (XV), December 19, 1960.
[24] "Issues Before the Sixteenth General Assembly," *International Conciliation*, No. 534 (September 1961), p. 81.

nation for Algeria in a French referendum. Talks between French officials and Algerian representatives led to conclusion of a cease-fire on March 19, 1962, followed by a referendum in Algeria in July. The majority of the Algerian people voted for independence with continued ties to France.

During the sixteenth General Assembly, the First Committee discussed the Algerian question at the request of thirty-three Afro-Asian states. A draft resolution of the First Committee recommended to the Assembly was adopted in plenary by a vote of 62 in favor, none against, with 38 abstaining (or 62-0-38). The resolution called for the two parties to resume negotiations "with a view to implementing the right of the Algerian people to self-determination and independence respecting the unity and territorial integrity of Algeria."[25] A final solution to the war developed out of bilateral negotiations, with the Organization serving as "an overt pressure group,"[26] urging the parties to find a solution to a protracted and increasingly costly colonial conflict.

Throughout the course of the Algerian war, additional pressures were exerted on the French through NATO. But the presence of the Portuguese and the British in the alliance mitigated the effects of these pressures. French allies, including the United States, exercised caution, especially after De Gaulle's attitude indicated a willingness to terminate the conflict. Ambiguity colored the remarks of Western delegates in the United Nations' political organs. The remaining colonial powers were anxious to avoid U.N. intrusion into the affairs

[25] General Assembly Resolution 1724 (XVI), December 20, 1961.
[26] Norman Palmer, "The Afro-Asians in the U.N.," in Franz Gross (ed.), *The United States and the United Nations* (Norman, Oklahoma: University of Oklahoma Press, 1964), p. 154.

of their territories; the United States did not want to alienate either the French or the Afro-Asian states that the Soviet Union desired to impress and influence.

The insurgents in the Indonesian and Algerian colonial wars made their cause heard at the United Nations through the medium of sympathetic third-party states. An important element of the arguments advanced in favor of U.N. endorsement of independence for Indonesia and Algeria was the stress placed on the "right of self-determination." The term "self-determination" appears in the United Nations' constitutional document in Articles 1 and 55 as a "principle" not as a "right," and refers to the "self-determination of peoples." The Charter provides no suggestions as to how the term "peoples" should be defined. Renewed interest in the status of self-determination as a "right" has been aroused by the Declaration on the Granting of Independence to Colonial Countries and Peoples,[27] adopted by the Assembly in 1960 prior to the outbreak of rebellion in Angola. The Declaration, passed by a vote of 89-0-9,[28] marked the culmination of Afro-Asian efforts to commit the entire membership of the United Nations to ending the institution of colonialism. The Declaration insisted that

> immediate steps shall be taken . . . to transfer all powers to the peoples of [dependent] territories, without any conditions or reservations, in accordance with their freely expressed will and desire, without any distinction as to race, creed or colour, in order to en-

[27] General Assembly Resolution 1514 (XV), December 14, 1960.
[28] Australia, Belgium, the Dominican Republic, France, Portugal, Spain, South Africa, the United Kingdom, and the United States abstained.

able them to enjoy complete independence and freedom; [that] all armed action or repressive measures
. . . directed against dependent peoples shall cease;
[and that] the integrity of their national territory
shall be respected.[29]

The Declaration has been cited in Assembly and
Council debate and has been mentioned in resolutions
on Angola. Supplementing the Declaration was agreement in the Fourth Committee and in plenary on twelve
principles clarifying the ambiguities of Chapter XI
of the Charter. These principles satisfied the Assembly's
immediate need for guidelines to judge Portugal's obligation to transmit information on Angola and other non-
self-governing territories under Article 73(e).[30] They
amplified the meaning of the phrase "full self-government" to include either "emergence as a sovereign state,"
"free association," or integration with an independent
state. They also provided that, when necessary, the
United Nations could supervise elections, plebiscites,
or referenda leading to a change in a territory's status.

The legal significance of the obligations outlined in
the Declaration is open to question. Rosalyn Higgins

[29] General Assembly Resolution 1514 (XV), December 14, 1960.

[30] Article 73(e) states: "Members of the United Nations which
have or assume responsibilities for the administration of territories
whose peoples have not yet attained a full measure of self-government recognize the principle that interests of the inhabitants of these
territories are paramount, and accept as a sacred trust the obligation
to promote to the utmost, within the system of international peace
and security established by the present Charter, the well-being of the
inhabitants of these territories, and to this end:

e. to transmit regularly to the Secretary-General for information
purposes, subject to such limitation as security and constitutional
considerations may require, statistical and other information of a
technical nature relating to economic, social, and educational conditions in the territories for which they are respectively responsible
other than those territories to which Chapter XII and XIII apply."

argues that passage of the Declaration by an over-whelming majority confirms that "a legal right of self-determination exists."[31] But the states to whom the Declaration is addressed primarily deny its obligatory character. Their eventual conformity to it is likely to result from political and economic pressures, just as the general approval of its tenets by the Assembly resulted from moral approbation in the light of political realities. The compliance of non-colonial powers cannot be accepted as a convincing test of the resolution's "legality." Other representatives expressed agreement with the Swedish delegate's explanation of his country's affirmative vote on the Declaration: "We understand it to be meant as a statement of general objectives and not as an act of legislation which would place immediate juridical obligations on Member States and which is designed to be applied literally."[32] Thus the passage of the Declaration has not altered the fact that "the right of self-determination has . . . no stable place in the international legal structure nor has it been accepted by states as a policy to be applied consistently and across the board."[33] Nevertheless, in the years since adoption of the Declaration, the African states have pressed for interpretations and additions that would force alterations in the policies of the remaining colonial powers.[34]

[31] Rosalyn Higgins, *The Development of International Law Through the Political Organs of the United Nations* (New York: Oxford University Press, 1963), pp. 95, 96, 181.

[32] U.N. Doc. A/P.V. 946, December 14, 1960, p. 7.

[33] Emerson, p. 306.

[34] On December 20, 1965, the Assembly passed a resolution [(2105) (XX)] requesting the Special Committee of 24 on the implementation of the Declaration to recommend a deadline for accession to independence of each territory, in accordance with the wishes of the people. The resolution also requested all states and international organizations to refuse to assist Portugal and South Africa so long as these

Angola

The differing attitudes of the Afro-Asian states, the Western powers, and the Soviet camp toward the Declaration have figured in the Organization's consideration of the Angolan colonial war. Since violence in Angola came to the attention of the Organization in 1961, the African states in the Assembly have successfully exploited the technique of continuing U.N. investigation in their efforts to embarrass and condemn Portugal in order to effect a change in her colonial policies. The Black African states, determined to eliminate a group of white regimes from their continent, have linked attacks on the Salazar government to those on the British in connection with Rhodesia and South Africa. The Council and Assembly have employed a combination of traditional resolutions and collective measures in order to encourage parties to the colonial war to resolve their differences without additional bloodshed. The Assembly has tried to promote an amelioration of conditions. Both political organs have urged member-states to use their influence to promote "peaceful" decolonization; both have consistently rejected challenges to their competence based on Portuguese readings of Article 2:7.

After the Security Council failed to approve a draft resolution calling for an inquiry into disturbances in

---

governments maintained policies of racial discrimination and "colonial domination." In addition, the resolution requested all colonial powers to dismantle existing military bases and to refrain from establishing new ones in territories under their control. The Special Committee was requested to submit information on any developments pursuant to the resolution that might threaten international peace and security. Seventy-four states voted in favor of the resolution; the United States, Britain, Australia, and New Zealand joined Portugal and South Africa in opposing it. Perhaps more significant than the predictable negative votes were the abstentions of 27 states.

Angola, the General Assembly, at the request of forty members, considered the matter and in April 1961 passed a resolution appointing an investigatory sub-committee,[35] comprising Bolivia, Dahomey, Malaya, Finland, and Sudan. In May 1961 the Angolan strife again came to the attention of the Security Council. In June the Council adopted a resolution in which it called upon Portuguese officials to "desist forthwith from repressive measures" and to facilitate the work of the Sub-Committee.[36] Although the Sub-Committee has not conducted interviews in the territory, it has implemented its mandate by submitting detailed reports to the Assembly. These reports have included strongly worded condemnation of Portugal for its "armed action and repressive measures against the Angolan people," and warnings that if the Portuguese government fails to heed U.N. resolutions "the situation in Angola will continue to deteriorate and become a more serious threat to international peace and security." The investigators have called on Portugal to recognize Angola's right of self-determination, to release political prisoners, and to enter into *pourparlers* with Angolan groups to ensure free elections and the eventual transfer of power.[37] The reports have included comments on political developments within the territory and excerpts from interviews with leaders of Angolan groups, individuals who refute Portuguese allegations of a "normal" situation. The Sub-Committee has stressed the non-cooperation of the Salazar government and the likely extension of the conflict

[35] General Assembly Resolution 1603 (XV), April 20, 1961.

[36] Security Council Resolution S/4835, June 9, 1961.

[37] See U.N. Doc. A/4978, Corr. 2, November 20, 1961, and General Assembly, *Official Records*, Sixteenth Session, 1088th-1102nd Meetings (January 15-30, 1962).

with continued non-compliance. The governmental representatives conducting the investigation have emphasized the powers of the Assembly and Council to consider further measures if Portuguese policies force a
deterioration of the situation. The findings of the Sub-
Committee on Angola would carry greater weight if investigators were permitted to visit the territory and to
conduct hearings there. Nevertheless, the reports of the
Sub-Committee have played a role in shaping the course
of the Organization's response to the colonial war. The
reports have confirmed the previously held opinions of
the African states and have helped to secure affirmative
votes in the Council and Assembly for collective action
against Portugal.

When Portugal failed to comply with resolutions calling for direct negotiations between the parties, the
Council, in July 1963, passed a more significant resolution establishing non-military collective measures in the
form of an arms embargo directed against Portugal.[38]
The same resolution insisted that Portugal acknowledge
the right of her colonies to independence and marked
the high point of the 32-nation African drive to compel
Salazar's retreat from Africa. Britain, France, and the
United States abstained. The Council's resolution did
not call for the Secretary-General or any organ of the
United Nations to initiate or direct the ban. Rather,
member-states were urged to adjust their national policies so as to exert additional pressures on Portugal. The
abstentions of major NATO powers, the chief arms sup-
pliers of Portugal, signified but a token acceptance of
the ban. Yet the abstentions were noteworthy; they
marked a shift from the earlier negative Assembly votes

[38] Security Council Resolution S/5380, July 31, 1963.

of Portugal's allies. The July resolution marked a compromise between the demands of African states for enforcement action against Portugal and the more moderate attitudes of other states. Brazil and Norway, who had abstained on a similar Assembly resolution the preceding December, thus voted in favor of the Council's July resolution. In December 1963 the American position shifted again, as the United States voted in favor of a Council resolution affirming the July arms ban. And the French government's delegate felt obliged to justify the continued French abstention on grounds that a broad consensus rather than a formal resolution would afford the best means of reopening talks between the parties.[39]

While rejecting Portugal's domestic jurisdiction claims and attempts to evade Article 73(e), the older Western states have shown themselves less comfortable with the notion of "the right of self-determination" African states advance at every turn in Assembly and Council debates. Yet without accepting the "legality" of this doctrine, the United States, and to a lesser extent Britain and France, have made political concessions within the United Nations to those states who argue for it. Thus, the December 1963 Council resolution, in addition to calling upon states to comply with the July arms embargo, suggested that an amnesty for those advocating self-determination for Angola would be evidence of good faith.[40]

The procedure of peaceful settlement stressed in the African-sponsored Assembly and Council resolutions on Angola is direct negotiations between the parties. These talks, initiated by the Secretary-General pursuant to

[39] Security Council, *Official Records*, Eighteenth Year, 1083rd Meeting (December 11, 1963), paras. 62-63.

[40] Security Council Resolution S/5480, December 11, 1963.

U.N. resolutions, have failed to produce notable concessions or compromises because, as Thant reported, the parties disagreed on the meaning of the term "self-determination."[41] While Portuguese authorities have promised new electoral laws designed to ensure local participation in administrative and political life "at all levels," Africans insist that Angola must be free to opt out of Portugal's control.

The formation of the Organization of African Unity in 1963 provided new impetus for a sanctionist approach to Portugal in the United Nations. After the unsuccessful U.N.-sponsored negotiations broke down in 1963, the African states expressed the view that the OAU should explore the possibility of further talks with Portugal. No progress has been recorded since that date. While individual African countries recognized Holden Roberto's exile government as the de jure authority in Angola and urged states to channel assistance to the rebels and to aid in their training, the rebels' fortunes have slipped as the war has continued. A lag in arms shipments and splits within the leadership of the rebel forces have combined to diminish the strength of the revolt. The African states have sought to keep the issues of Portugal's non-compliance with U.N. resolutions before the Security Council, despite the dwindling of organized violence in Angola. On November 23, 1965, the Council concluded a series of eight meetings in which familiar allegations and refutations were exchanged with passage of a resolution reaffirming previous resolutions on Angola and calling upon Portugal "to give immediate effect to the principle of self-determination."[42]

[41] See U.N. Doc. S/5448 and Add. 1-3, October 31, 1963, especially para. 11.

[42] See U.N. Doc. S/6953, November 18, 1965, para. 4.

The Council also repeated its demand that Portugal engage in negotiations "on the basis of the recognition of the right of self-determination"[43] looking toward a transfer of power to indigenous groups.

Limited fact-finding under U.N. auspices has exposed the repressive character of Portugal's administration in Angola and has sparked a partial modification of Salazar's official policies. But these concessions lie in the realm of tactics, not strategy. The important changes brought about by U.N.-centered African pressures have occurred in the public position of the United States, Britain, and France. Pressures brought to bear on Portugal's allies and in turn on that colonial state are responsible for Salazar's minor gestures of conciliation. These pressures, stressed in Council resolutions, have been applied outside the United Nations. As a colonial war on the Algerian model rather than a post-colonial conflict along Congo lines, with a viable, if increasingly isolated, entrenched regime in power, the Angolan colonial war is less susceptible to the imposition of an outside political settlement engineered by interested third parties in the context of regional or international institutions. Combined bilateral and multilateral pressures may result in a less intransigent Portuguese attitude, but the details of a transition from colonial rule to full self-rule for Angola are likely to be hammered out by the parties themselves rather than by officials of interested outside organizations.

Conclusion

Despite their avowed intentions to retain control over their colonial possessions, the Dutch, French, and Por-

[43] *Ibid.*, para. 5.

tuguese governments proved susceptible to pressures brought to bear on them by states in the councils of the United Nations and in the context of bilateral relations. The United Nations served as a forum for the expression of anti-colonialist sentiments in the Algerian colonial war for years before a final solution was worked out by the parties themselves. The political solutions to colonial wars which have engaged the attention of the United Nations since 1946 were arranged when the colonial states realized that their policies had become increasingly dysfunctional. Although the final chapter in the Angolan colonial war remains to be written, it is conceivable that a post-Salazar regime in Portugal may arrive at a decision to divest itself of colonies as did the French and Dutch earlier.

In the Indonesian, Algerian, and Angolan cases, the Organization did not undertake courses of action requiring massive or continuing U.N. responsibilities, or arousing the implacable hostility of permanent members of the Security Council. The colonial powers vociferously opposed U.N. discussion or action as prejudicial to the maintenance of their authority, but when the administering states have realized that their goals are incapable of realization, they have had the opportunity to use the United Nations to let it appear that they were being compelled to make otherwise unacceptable compromises or concessions. A locus of governmental authority remained in Indonesia, Algeria, and Angola to which U.N. resolutions could be addressed and against which multilateral, bilateral, or regional economic and political pressures could be directed.

The often uncomfortable middle-man position the United States has adopted in the Organization's handling of colonial wars allowed the United States to support resolutions urging an end to hostilities and the transfer of power in Indonesia, to abstain from some resolutions while directing bilateral pressures in Algeria and Angola, and finally to approve African-sponsored resolutions calling for collective measures against Portugal and negotiations looking toward eventual Angolan independence. The Soviet Union has attempted to play the role of protector of the new states against the Western colonial powers. The interest in extending Russian influence in the third world has led the Soviets to support the far-reaching draft resolutions of the African states in Algeria and Angola. The Soviet Union has avoided the dilemmas faced by American officials in Indonesia and later in Algeria and Angola, dilemmas arising from the U.S. desires to placate military allies while at the same time appearing to endorse the claims of non-white peoples for independence.

For the newer states, whose membership in the United Nations has set the seal on their independence, the Organization has served as an important diplomatic instrument, permitting continuous contact with larger states whose developmental aid is sought and providing an open forum in which demands for an end to the remaining vestiges of colonial rule may be aired. The colonial disorders are questions on which the newer states are in agreement.

The Assembly and Council, led by the increasing majority of these newer states, have accepted interpretations of colonial disorders as threats not only to regional stability but to international peace and security. The political organs have taken a broad view of the United Nations' competence to discuss and take action in colonial wars. But the effectiveness of Council and Assembly resolutions has depended on the susceptibility of incumbents and insurgents to bilateral pressures. The linking of "the right of self-determination" with "the right of revolution" has raised crucial questions for individuals and member-states involved in the state-building and nation-building processes attending internal conflicts. What degree of political maturity is required to justify the invocation of a right of self-determination before an international organization's political councils? Should the right of self-determination extend to secessionist groups who wish to opt out of a state structure imposed by outside authorities as a condition of independence, a state structure reflecting non-indigenous political traditions and cultures ill-suited to local demands? These questions have been posed not only in the Organization's consideration of colonial wars erupting before an initial transfer of power is completed but also in post-colonial conflicts. These "delayed-reaction" conflicts have been waged by indigenous groups, with outside participation, by local rivals for power whose confrontation was avoided earlier by the presence of an entrenched governmental authority. Despite the differences in the colonial and post-colonial conflicts, the Organization's primary concern with threats to international peace and security has resulted in similar international preoccupation with outcomes, regardless of the immediate origins of conflict.

The relatively uncomplicated role played by the United Nations in the Indonesian, Algerian, and Angolan cases contrasts sharply with the intricacies of its prolonged involvement in the Congo's political affairs and the Cyprus dispute, to be examined, together with the Dominican internal conflict, in Chapter 3. These disorders have confronted the Organization with an array of parties whose interests transcend the pattern suggested by the terms "incumbents" and "insurgents." The Indonesian, Algerian, and Angolan conflicts came to the Organization before the colonial powers had made known what specific procedures they intended to follow in altering the status of territories. There were opportunities for U.N. political bodies to express a preference for suitable procedures to be used in the transfer of power. The United Nations' pro-Western majority supported the establishment of an independent Indonesia rather than the union originally offered by the Dutch. The Afro-Asian states have furnished numerous proposals for the type of political structure they favor in Angola. In the Algerian conflict the De Gaulle government worked out its own procedures and schedule for the transition, once an acceptance of the inevitability of independence became widespread in the metropole and among the bulk of European settlers in the colony. The Organization did not undertake to suggest details of the political arrangements to follow Algerian-French hostilities since the Western powers and others did not wish to jeopardize chances for a solution. In the Congo, Cyprus, and Dominican disorders, the Organization has faced problems of internal instability whose origins are to be found in a lack of adequate preparation for self-rule. Thus the onus of failure in these cases rests with colonizing states, with involved regional institutions, and, in some instances, with individual political leaders whose actions or inaction preceded U.N. involvement in shaping the political structures of these states.

CHAPTER III

The United Nations Role in Internal Conflicts Involving a Breakdown of Law and Order

IN its efforts to promote political solutions to the problems posed by the outbreak of hostilities in the Congo, Cyprus, and Dominican cases, the United Nations has sought to restore and maintain international peace and security, pursuant to its principles and purposes. The Organization has tried to prevent external interventions from escalating local violence into cold-war conflagrations. Its ability to realize these goals has been limited by the inadequacy of means available and by the attitudes of member-states with national interests in the outcome of internal strife. These limitations have also plagued the United Nations efforts in attempts to realize similar goals in colonial wars and in internal disorders involving charges of external aggression or subversion. But special difficulties have accompanied the Organization's efforts in internal disorders involving a breakdown of law and order. Despite the differences in the political development of the Congo, Cyprus, and the Dominican Republic prior to the onset of internal strife, each country has suffered from the absence of viable indigenous governmental institutions through which representative political authority could be exercised. Decades of Belgian colonial administration in the Congo, British, Greek, and Turkish control in Cyprus, and Trujillo's personal rule in the Dominican Republic did little to prepare the way for peaceful self-government. The breakdown of law and order in these countries has exposed the weaknesses of the social fabric in developing societies with minority groups of a mixed racial or linguistic heritage. Moreover, the participation of regional organizations in the Congo, Cyprus, and Dominican disorders has created political and legal issues of greater complexity than those encountered in the Organization's involvement in colonial wars.

The U.N. role in the Congo, Cyprus, and Dominican disorders is of particular significance in view of the possibility of future breakdowns in other African, Latin American, Asian, or Middle Eastern countries. The extensive U.N. field missions in the Congo and Cyprus, if analyzed apart from a context in which other internal disorders are discussed, may lead observers to emphasize the uniqueness of the problems faced by the Organization in each case. Insofar as a breakdown of law and order may be regarded as a potential threat in any developing society, it is useful to examine the Organization's handling of the two cases in a broad perspective rather than within the narrower confines of post-colonialism or U.N. peace-keeping operations. The effectiveness of the Organization in coping with future disorders that may require a protracted consensus and involve a commitment to a particular outcome may be clarified and the importance, as a possible precedent, of its limited role in the Dominican strife may be judged.

The Congo

The admission of newly independent, politically inexperienced African states into the United Nations after 1958 did not prepare the Organization for the widespread upheaval touched off in the Congo by the *Force Publique*'s mutiny six days after the Belgians' hasty grant of independence on June 30, 1960. For four years, against a background of chronic instability and tribal warfare, U.N. administrators sought to control violence in the new state and to foster national unification among political regimes or individuals backed by outside states. Bilateral techniques and pressures and good offices under national, regional, and international auspices failed to promote a lasting political solution to the Congo's difficulties. The vast area's appalling lack of preparation for self-rule—the paucity of trained personnel in public administration, economic affairs, health, and other basic services—is still an impediment; despite extensive state-building and state-preserving activities under U.N. aegis,[1] the former Belgian colony represents diversified interests, tribal allegiances, and external pressures; it has ambivalent relations to the metropole, the superpowers, and neighboring post-colonial entities in Africa. If a nation is defined as a community coterminus with the boundaries of a state commanding the loyalties of the majority of its inhabitants, the Congo cannot be said to have achieved nationhood.

The problems which were to beset officials of the United Nations engaged in peace-keeping and extensive civilian operations in the Congo had roots in pre-independence politics. The series of events bringing into direct confrontation the forces of nationalism, colonialism, and ideological antagonism began well before June 30, 1960. Although the economic advancement of the Congolese placed them far ahead of their African counterparts in British colonies like Northern Rhodesia, their lack of political experience, their lack of training in the procedures of government and politics, proved to be an

[1] See Harold Jacobson, "ONUC's Civilian Operations: State-Building and State-Preserving," *World Politics*, xvii (October 1964), 75-107.

67

enormous handicap when the Belgians agreed to yield to demands of local groups for immediate independence. Abandoning a gradualist approach to decolonization, the Belgians accepted proposals for a transfer of power put forward at a round-table conference held six months before Independence Day. Separatist tendencies were readily apparent at this conference, which was attended by sixty-two Congolese, representing twenty parties, and nineteen others, representing tribes.[2] In May 1960 the Belgian government issued the *Loi Fondamentale*,[3] which was to serve as the basis for the Congo's constitution after independence. This incredibly complex and lengthy document, containing 259 articles, flew in the face of the one clear reality of Congolese political life— the inability of one tribe or one party to muster enough support to rule effectively. Elections held for seats to the new provisional assemblies and the National Chamber of Deputies showed that no individual or party had a firm majority. But Nkrumah's influence enabled a national government to be formed with two rival politicians—Kasavubu and Lumumba—linked in a coalition regime.

The Belgians not only failed to provide the Congolese with training in high-level governmental administration prior to independence, they also failed to pre-

[2] For a discussion of the political background of the Brussels Conference, see Colin Legum, *Congo Disaster* (Baltimore: Penguin, 1961), pp. 73-85. For material on pre-independence politics in the Congo, see Alan Merriam, *Congo: Background of Conflict* (Evanston: Northwestern University Press, 1961), pp. 29-65; Fernand Van Langenhove, *The Congo and Problems of Decolonization* (Brussels: Institut Royal des Relations Internationales, 1960), pp. 1-26.

[3] For a detailed discussion of the history of the Fundamental Law, see Herbert J. Spiro, *Politics in Africa* (Englewood Cliffs: Prentice Hall, 1964), pp. 120-122.

pare their colonial peoples for economic management or leadership positions in education. Of greater consequence in the days immediately following independence was the Belgian policy of limiting the officer corps in the *Force Publique* to Europeans. When the *Force* was renamed the Congolese National Army (ANC—Armée Nationale Congolaise), no corresponding alterations in the command structure were made. On July 5th, following tribal violence in Leopoldville and Luluabourg, Congolese soldiers rose against their Belgian superiors. When Lumumba refused to allow metropolitan Belgian troops to restore order (they were stationed at two bases under the provisions of the Treaty of Friendship concluded before independence), the Belgians left Kitona and Kamina on July 10th and moved into several Congolese cities. Whatever discipline remained in the ANC disintegrated rapidly.[4]

Prior to the July 5th uprising, U.N. Undersecretary Ralph Bunche and Congolese officials had discussed the possibility of U.N. military assistance in retraining the *Force Publique*. Through responsibilities placed upon him by the Council and Assembly and his own diplomatic initiatives in UNEF,[5] UNOGIL, and other instances, Hammarskjöld had enhanced his own personal prestige among delegates as well as the power of the office he held. Therefore it was natural that member-states should look to the Secretariat, specifically to Hammarskjöld, for guidance on the suitable course for the Organization to pursue when, on July 13th, Congolese

[4] For additional details, see Ernest Lefever, *Crisis in the Congo: A United Nations Force in Action* (Washington: The Brookings Institution, 1965), pp. 6-13.

[5] See Gabriella Rosner, *The United Nations Emergency Force* (New York: Columbia University Press, 1963).

authorities appealed directly to the Secretary-General for U.N. military aid, after the American government had rejected a similar request.[6] It was also natural that when the Security Council decided to undertake collective action in response to the severe breakdown of law and order in the new state that Hammarskjöld should be entrusted with executive responsibilities.

The July 11th announcement of the secession of Katanga Province by its President, Moise Tshombe, dramatized the inadequacies of the Belgian-drafted *Loi Fondamentale* and the fragile basis of support for the Leopoldville coalition regime of Lumumba and Kasavubu. The Government's cable to Hammarskjöld on July 12th had charged Belgium with responsibility for the secession, calling it a "conspiracy" and "a disguised perpetuation of the colonialist regime."[7] The Kasavubu-Lumumba telegram to the Secretary-General emphasized the "illegal" Belgian actions in violation of the Treaty of Friendship concluded just prior to independence. Hammarskjöld convened the Council to consider the new government's request for U.N. military assistance. He later explained his first use of Article 99 in terms emphasizing the need for prompt U.N. action:

[6] Several reasons for the American decision to urge U.N. action in the Congo's affairs rather than to intervene bilaterally are mentioned by Ernest Lefever in "The U.N. as a Foreign Policy Instrument: The Congo Crisis," in Roger Hilsman and Robert C. Good (eds.), *Foreign Policy in the Sixties: The Issues and the Instruments* (Baltimore: Johns Hopkins Press, 1965), pp. 141-157. Lefever cites three motives favoring U.N. participation rather than a U.S. unilateral military presence; first, the desire of American officials to achieve stability without alienating the new African states; second, the desire to avoid a major U.S. military commitment on that continent; and third, the desire to strengthen the peace-keeping capability of the U.N.

[7] U.N. Doc. S/4382, July 13, 1960, p. 2.

the breakdown of law and order created a situation which through its consequences had imposed a threat to peace and security justifying United Nations intervention. . . . whether or not it was also held that the U.N. faced a conflict between two parties was, under the circumstances, in my view, legally not essential for the justification of the action.[8]

Anxious to avoid having the Congo difficulties drawn into cold-war politics, Hammarskjöld played down aspects that might have supported the Russian-inspired drive to apply enforcement measures under Articles 41 or 42[9] against Belgium.

In his remarks to the Council prior to the adoption of the first resolution on the Congo, the Secretary-General stressed that he would be guided by principles developed in the UNEF operation. In keeping with the pacific procedures employed in the establishment of U.N. military forces in the Suez crisis, the proposed Congo force would consist of troop contingents drawn from small and "middle" states, with the permanent members of the Security Council excluded from participation. The disorders in the Congo at the time of the first resolution

---

[8] U.N. Doc. S/4389, July 18, 1960, p. 2.

[9] Article 41 states: "The Security Council may decide what measures not involving the use of armed force are to be employed to give effect to its decisions, and it may call upon the Members of the United Nations to apply such measures. These may include complete or partial interruption of economic relations and of rail, sea, air, postal, telegraphic, radio, and other means of communication, and the severance of diplomatic relations."

Article 42 states: "Should the Security Council consider that measures provided for in Article 41 would be inadequate or have proved to be inadequate, it may take such action by air, sea, or land forces as may be necessary to maintain or restore international peace and security. Such action may include demonstrations, blockade, and other operations by air, sea, or land forces of Members of the United Nations."

had not taken on the character of full-scale civil war; on the basis of the information available, the Security Council supported Hammarskjöld's proposals. Clearly, the Western powers were not prepared to call for "enforcement" action against Belgium, and neither superpower wished to see forces of the other positioned in the unstable African country.

In its first resolution on the Congo, the Council "called upon" Belgium to withdraw its troops from the Congo but did not cite Articles 39 or 40 explicitly. The order of priorities the Secretary-General emphasized in his remarks to the Council was incorporated in the resolution of July 14th sponsored by Tunisia:[10] Belgian withdrawal from the Congo's territory and dispatch of military assistance to the Central Government to "enable national security forces to meet their tasks.[11] The resolution, empowering the Secretary-General, rather than member-states, to "take steps" to render the distressed government aid, revealed the assumptions of members and the Secretary-General that a temporary security force of moderate proportions would suffice to restore order in the Congo after the withdrawal of Belgian troops. Behind the resolution lay additional assumptions: that the Belgian government would withdraw its forces as soon as the U.N. Force could become operational; that the Congo's civilian administration (with U.N. assistance) could exercise its direction over the mutinous army; and that the Congolese authorities could work out their own constitutional arrangements for Katanga and other dis-

[10] The U.S., the U.S.S.R., Argentina, Ceylon, Ecuador, Poland, Italy, and Tunisia voted for the resolution; China, Britain, and France abstained.

[11] Security Council Resolution S/4387, July 14, 1960.

sident provinces. No member-state attempted to place cost or time limitations on the proposed Force; indeed the use of the term "United Nations Force" was specifically excluded from the first resolution.

The initial recruitment and dispatch of the new Force was accomplished smoothly.[12] By July 31, 1960, ONUC, consisting of 11,155 troops from seven African nations and one European country, was deployed in all Congo provinces save Katanga. What Hammarskjöld described as the "biggest single effort under United Nations colors organized and directed by the U.N. itself"[13] had begun its controversial existence.

Definition of ONUC's functions and powers proceeded in Council debates prior to the Council's second and third resolutions of July 22nd and August 9th. The July 22nd resolution, adopted unanimously, called upon Belgium to "implement speedily" the withdrawal of its troops.[14] The August 9th resolution called upon Belgium to withdraw its troops from Katanga and authorized the entry of ONUC into the rebel province.[15] While the latter resolution did not change the character of the Force, it was notable for its mention of Articles 25 and 49.[16]

[12] Within twenty-four hours, General von Horn had arrived in Leopoldville from Gaza to take command of troops sent from Ghana, Guinea, Morocco, and Tunisia, troops promised to the Secretary-General before the July 14th resolution. After four days, 3,500 men were deployed in Leopoldville, Stanleyville, Matadi, Thysville, and Coquilhatville. Combat troops from India, Ethiopia, Ireland, Nigeria, Sweden, and Liberia followed. Auxiliary units, including air transport and medical corps from Pakistan, Canada, Italy, Norway, Denmark, Argentina, Greece, Brazil, Ceylon, Netherlands, Austria, and Ecuador, plus riot police from Nigeria joined the collective effort.

[13] U.N. Doc. S/P.V. 877, July 20, 1960, p. 8.

[14] Security Council Resolution S/4405, July 22, 1960.

[15] Security Council Resolution S/4424, August 9, 1960. France and Italy abstained.

[16] Article 25 states: "The Members of the United Nations agree to

The Council upheld Hammarskjöld's interpretations of the prior July resolutions: The United Nations could neither interfere in the Central Government's relation to Katanga nor undertake military operations against the secessionist province. In keeping with UNEF principles, Hammarskjöld had insisted from the beginning of the United Nations' concern with the Congo that the new Force would not become a party to internal conflicts. The Organization's operation in the Congo as set forth in the first three Council resolutions was thus conceived as fulfilling the essentially negative task of preventing escalation by (1) securing the withdrawal of Belgian troops, (2) restoring law and order, and (3) ensuring respect for the territorial integrity and political independence of the Congo. The reactions of U.N. officialdom to the political confusion in the Congo following the breakdown of law and order and the establishment of ONUC indicated that constitutional issues would be handled as a separate problem to be solved by the Congolese themselves.

Whatever the apparent relevance of UNEF for ONUC in the recruitment of men and matériel, it became clear in the summer and autumn of 1960 that the vacuum left by the flight of Belgian civilian personnel, coupled with Katanga's secession and the tendency of each Congolese leader to solicit aid from foreign powers useful to his own political ends, confronted the United Nations with a situation wholly different from

---

accept and carry out the decisions of the Security Council in accordance with the present Charter."

Article 49 states: "The Members of the United Nations shall join in affording mutual assistance in carrying out the measures decided upon by the Security Council."

that of Suez in 1956. As Ruth Russell has remarked, the effectiveness of U.N. peace-keeping operations "is in almost mathematical proportion to the degree of political accord that underlies them."[17] The minimal consensus that had made ONUC a reality in July began to shift in August and September 1960, as it would in other critical moments of ONUC's history. Continuing disorder in the Congo challenged the principles and assumptions underlying ONUC's initiation and administration, principles and assumptions drawn from the Organization's previous experiences in Suez and Lebanon.

As the national interests of the superpowers in the Congo became clarified, the fluid positions of the major powers that permitted passage of the July and August Council resolutions hardened. Soviet support for Lumumba during disorders in Kasai and American support for Kasavubu as the more moderate figure of the Leopoldville group were mirrored in Council debate.[18] Thus in August, the Soviet Union and Poland, expressing satisfaction with the idea of a non-intervention policy, maintained that the conflict between Leopoldville and Katanga could not be considered an internal disorder in view of Belgian support for Tshombe, hence the non-intervention posture suitable for the United Nations in internal matters should not apply. At this stage of the United Nations' involvement in the Congo, both superpowers were willing to approve or reaffirm ambiguous measures so long as they could be re-evaluated in the clearer light of national-policy considerations when problems of implementation arose. No major pow-

[17] Quoted in *The New York Times*, July 5, 1964.
[18] American endorsement secured the seating of Kasavubu's representatives in the Assembly on November 22, 1960, over Soviet and African protests.

er regarded ONUC as a substitute for its own diplomacy.

Vague mandates in New York invited conflicting interpretations in the major capitals and in the field. Increasingly, implementation of Council resolutions required a delicate juggling of the demands of rival Congolese politicians. Hammarskjöld's treatment of the military and political aspects of the Congo conflict in August 1960 reflected his belief that the United Nations' police role could be separated from its conciliation function. The Secretary-General's conception of priorities prevailed as he sought to obtain freedom of movement for ONUC throughout the entire Congo, including the rebel province of Katanga, pursuant to the July 22nd and August 9th Council resolutions. In the Secretary-General's view, the presence of Belgian personnel favorable to the continued secession would hinder any chances for conciliation and a political settlement. Hammarskjöld attempted to maintain his conception of priorities after many Belgians returned to Leopoldville in October 1960, when the Congolese Army's General Mobutu and his youthful commissioners had taken power:

> . . . if we could fully circumscribe the Belgian factor and eliminate it, we could lay the groundwork for a reconciliation of Katanga and the rest of the territory of the Republic of the Congo, [and] the situation in Leopoldville might well be rectified.[19]

But as Soviet attacks on Hammarskjöld and his office began to mount and the African consensus in the Assembly began to crumble after Lumumba's ouster in September, the Secretary-General found it difficult to

---

[19] U.N. Doc. S/4557, Part B, No. 5, November 2, 1960.

maintain a rigorous order of priorities for the Congo operation. His conception of the non-intervention posture of ONUC provoked an acrimonious controversy with Lumumba in August. Hammarskjöld's conviction that ONUC's original mandate prohibited the Force from engaging in joint operations with the forces of the Central Government alienated Lumumba, who had hoped to use ONUC as a substitute for the Congolese Army (ANC) in quelling Katanga. The Secretary-General stressed that the entry of ONUC into Katanga, postponed for three days until the Council could provide him with a mandate that would permit ONUC to deploy within the rebel province, was not to be interpreted as permitting subjugation of the province to the Central Government. Hammarskjöld aroused Lumumba's ire by refusing to permit ONUC to transport Central Government officials to Katanga and by failing to uphold the *Loi Fondamentale.* Insulting letters sent by Lumumba to Hammarskjöld further damaged opportunities for cordial relations between the host government and ONUC representatives.

The Secretary-General, as Hammarskjöld observed, may be the only international agent capable of dealing impartially and authoritatively with all parties to a dispute, but, unlike a national political figure, the Secretary-General possesses no constituency. The disaffection of a major power can destroy tenuous alignments in the Organization's political organs and adversely affect the chances for a pacific settlement of a particular situation. In order to place the plethora of political decisions taken in New York and in the Congo itself on a firmer footing, Hammarskjöld, in August 1960, had formed an advisory committee composed of representatives of the eighteen states contributing to ONUC. While Hammarskjöld and later Thant were to praise the work of the Advisory Committee, its ability to operate as an organ of conciliation as well as a source of guidance was circumscribed by the information it received. One critic asserts that as the Congo crisis deepened in 1960, the information gap widened:

> What produced the sense of shock was the growing impression that neither the General Assembly nor the Security Council had the full materials necessary for informed discussion, and adequately motivated decisions on the U.N. operation in the Congo. The only people who had these materials were the people who saw the actual telegrams—the inner circle of the Secretariat together with those, whoever they might be, to whom these telegrams might be shown from time to time by one of his principal advisers. As for the Congo Advisory Committee, "advising" the Secretary-General on the basis of the information with which the Secretary-General saw fit to supply it, it seemed in the light of the telegrams much less like an advisory body than a group of innocent outsiders being taken for a guided tour.[20]

The Advisory Committee's role as a buffer should not be underestimated, however. By the fall of 1960 such a buffer was needed. As the largest economic and military factor in the Congo, ONUC had become a stake in the conflicts among the leaders in Leopoldville, Stanleyville, and Elizabethville. At the same time, working relations between U.N. field personnel and Congolese de

[20] Conor Cruise O'Brien, *To Katanga and Back* (New York: Simon and Schuster, 1962), p. 50.

facto and de jure authorities steadily deteriorated. U.N.
field representatives were unable to repair the unsatisfactory relations obtaining first with the Kasavubu-Lumumba government and later with the Mobutu incumbents. Cordier's decision to close the radio station and
the airport on September 5th, at the height of the Kasavubu-Lumumba controversy, showed that every act or
omission of ONUC or its civilian personnel could affect
relations between factional leaders throughout the Congo and their foreign backers, as well as relations between U.N. representatives and local officials. Cordier's
replacement, Dayal, an experienced negotiator who had
served in Lebanon, withheld recognition from Mobutu's
commissioners and chose to deal with second-level officers. The ensuing friction, culminating in Dayal's recall
in the spring of 1961, threatened to poison feelings between U.N. administrators and Congolese leaders. Thus
non-intervention as a philosophical position had little
operational value in the Congo itself, where, as Dayal
observed, "almost every significant measure taken by
ONUC in the impartial fulfillment of its mandate had
been interpreted by one faction or another as being
directed against itself."[21]

There were several ways in which dissatisfied members could express annoyance with Hammarskjöld's
management of ONUC. States could vote against U.N.
resolutions, they could withhold funds for the Force,
they could vilify the executive and administrative officials connected with ONUC, and they could sabotage
field missions by means of their proxies on the scene, by
withdrawing or threatening to withdraw troop contingents or logistical support. These methods were em-

[21] U.N. Doc. S/4557, November 2, 1960.

ployed frequently by various states from September 1960 to February 1961.

In September 1960 the failure of Council members to approve American and Soviet draft resolutions and a compromise resolution sponsored by Tunisia and Ceylon led to a convening of the Assembly in emergency session under the Uniting for Peace Resolution. The divergent views recorded in the Council were echoed in the Assembly. Nevertheless, a resolution sponsored by seventeen Afro-Asian states was adopted without negative votes on September 20th.[22] The resolution, supporting Hammarskjöld's actions, was notable for its inclusion of a request that all states direct aid to the Congo through U.N. channels, and its appeal to all Congolese groups to resolve their internal conflicts "with the assistance, as appropriate, of Asian and African representatives appointed by the Advisory Committee on the Congo, in consultation with the Secretary-General, for the purpose of conciliation."[23]

In the months between September 20th and February 21, 1961, neither the Council nor the Assembly was able to agree on additional resolutions on the Congo disorders, despite the fact that events in the field made it clear that the guiding principles of the operation were inconsistent with each other and with the nature of the disorders the U.N. field personnel were attempting to ease. Questions arose that required further clarification of ONUC's mandate: Could ONUC, under the rubric of "military assistance" to the Central Government, interpose itself between the disorganized ANC and the civil-

[22] General Assembly Resolution 1474 Rev. 1 (ES-IV), September 20, 1960.

[23] *Ibid.*, para. 3.

ian population? Should the Force protect all Congolese leaders regardless of their relationship to the Leopoldville authorities? How far should ONUC's protection extend? Could action be taken against the Central Government if it violated the status-of-forces agreement or informal agreements negotiated by field personnel in order to give effect to Council resolutions? Could ONUC remain aloof from internal conflicts and still promote respect for the Congo's territorial integrity and political independence in the face of Katanga's continued secession? By February 1961 it was evident that reconciliation of Congolese factions along lines set forth in conflicting provisions of the August 9th and September 20th resolutions had failed. Field officials had demonstrated the unworkability of non-intervention as a guiding precept: "in practice every day they were taking decisions implying the use of U.N. forces in ways capable of influencing the internal affairs and the political future of the Congo, nor was it possible for them to do otherwise."[24]

Thus ONUC reached a turning point. The situation in the field—the continued constitutional crisis, secession, and indiscipline of the ANC—indicated that temporary interposition on the UNEF model was inadequate to the task the United Nations faced in the Congo. Other assumptions at the root of the Council's decision to organize the Force required revision. While the Assembly's September resolution had vindicated Hammarskjöld's actions, by February the unsavory circumstances surrounding Lumumba's death had aroused additional criticism from Soviet and African leaders. Important

[24] O'Brien, *To Katanga and Back*, p. 60.

choices had to be faced if the mission were to remain in the Congo. For, it had become obvious that

> The promotion of law and order in a setting of domestic factionalism is not compatible with the idea of neutrality and impartiality. It requires that a choice be made among competing prescriptions for law and order and competing candidates for the order-giving function.[25]

The Council could withdraw the Force from the Congo, leaving the country prey to externally abetted civil war, a more dangerous condition than July's domestic anarchy; or the Council could agree to go beyond the interposition concept by allowing ONUC more initiative in the promotion of a political settlement and in the use of force vis-à-vis principal disputants. The Council also could consider a change in the executive direction of ONUC. Guinea, Morocco, and the United Arab Republic had withdrawn contingents from ONUC, and others had announced plans to follow suit. Entangled in a web of political, logistical, and economic problems, ONUC faced its gravest threat—civil war and complete breakdown of law and order—at a time when its numbers were seriously depleted.

In the Security Council debate prior to adoption of the February resolution, the Soviet Union extended its attack on Hammarskjöld's direction of ONUC. Other states, again rejecting Russian suggestions that the United Nations apply sanctions against Belgium under Article 41, and that the Council set a one-month time limit for ONUC's termination, nevertheless were disturbed by Hammarskjöld's "too narrow legality" in the

---

[25] Claude, "The United Nations and the Use of Force," p. 379.

interpretation of Council and Assembly directives. The Secretary-General insisted that a new mandate was needed, that the Council "cannot shirk its responsibilities by expecting from the Secretariat action on which it is not prepared to take decisions itself."[26] Replying to Soviet criticism of his handling of Lumumba's capture, Hammarskjöld argued,

> The United Nations had neither the power nor the right to liberate Mr. Lumumba from his captors by force—I say the United Nations because to my knowledge not even this Council or the General Assembly could have such a right, much less did it exist for the U.N. representatives in the Congo under this mandate.[27]

Other interested parties agreed that ONUC's mandate should be reviewed, though there were apparent differences of opinion as to which "prescription for order" in the Congo should be followed, if indeed such a prescription could be found. American and Soviet disagreement over the United Nations' policies in the Congo could be expected, but splits between the various African states were to prove equally harmful to efforts to resolve the Congo's difficulties. The cleavage between the Brazzaville and Casablanca groups of African states stemmed from their different attitudes toward Tshombe. For the former French colonies, Tschombe seemed to be the most stable element in the turbulent political scene and could be regarded as a bulwark against Communist intrusion into Africa. These states were critical of ONUC, for they feared that the Force might set a

[26] Security Council, *Official Records*, Sixteenth Year, 935th Meeting (February 15, 1961), para. 35.

[27] *Ibid.*, para. 10.

dangerous precedent if military action were used to crush the Katangese President. In Andrew Boyd's opinion,

> Many Afro-Asians were, I think, cautious about creating precedents for U.N. action in domestic conflict cases. In the various discussions about U.N. forces there had always been a marked Afro-Asian caution, arising, one supposes, basically from fear of "neo-imperialist" use of the U.N. in weak newly-independent states. The Communist countries share, even foster this attitude of caution.[28]

The Brazzaville group itself split later at the sixteenth session of the Assembly. As regards ONUC in early 1961, the Casablanca states, a loose grouping of African nations led by Ghana and Guinea, were more sympathetic to Soviet attitudes. Advocating the opposite of a cautious attitude toward Tshombe, Nkrumah pressed for strong action to eliminate the rebel leader. He feared that a successful revolt of a Congolese province from the Central Government might lead to U.N. sanctification of African separatist movements that could engulf his own one-party state.[29] As early as September 1960, Nkrumah had warned that the United Nations' non-intervention posture in the Congo conflict would prove disastrous:

> The United Nations need not go to the assistance of any country which invites its intervention but once it does so it owes an obligation to the government and the people of that country not to interfere in such

[28] Andrew Boyd, quoted in O'Brien, *To Katanga and Back*, p. 89.
[29] See John Spencer, "Africa at the U.N.," *International Organization*, xvi (Spring 1962), 375ff.

a way as to prevent the legitimate government which invited it to enter the country from fulfilling its mandate. In other words, it is impossible for the U.N. at one and the same time to preserve law and order and to be neutral between the legal authorities and the law-breakers. That is, unfortunately, exactly what the U.N. has attempted to do in the Congo and that is the cause of all the present difficulties and disagreements.[30]

Having secured independence and self-determination for their countries, Nkrumah and Touré were determined to consolidate a favorable political and territorial status quo in Africa. They stressed that the Congo conflict threatened to undermine the basis for stability on the African continent.

The diplomatic isolation that was to mark Soviet conduct during ONUC's four years had taken form by February 1961. As the United States had become committed to the fortunes of Kasavubu and the series of Leopoldville functionaries, the Soviet Union groped for a proxy figure popular enough to challenge the American-backed Central Government. Lumumba's downfall narrowed the choice to Antoine Gizenga, whose lack of popular support impaired Russian strategy in the Congo. Within the United Nations, the Soviet delegate dubbed Tshombe Belgium's "lackey" and attempted to portray Khrushchev as the personal guardian of all new states against the colonial powers. Quick to denounce American domination of ONUC, the Russians developed a conspiracy theory to explain Belgian involvement in Katanga. The Soviets were irked that no Russian dele-

[30] General Assembly, *Official Records*, Fifteenth Session, 869th Plenary Meeting (September 23, 1960), p. 62, para. 17.

gate or official was party to the inner workings of the Secretariat's Congo club, which consisted of a Nigerian, an Englishman, an Indian, and three Americans. But the Soviets had no success in winning acceptance for their troika proposals or other plans that would have altered the executive direction of the Force. Significantly, the Russians, although maligning the Congo operation, did not counter it with massive unilateral aid, which might have antagonized those smaller states still supporting Hammarskjöld. Russian behavior in the Congo turmoil recalls similar behavior in the Spanish civil war: conflict with the international organization, failure to defy it completely, and reluctance to involve itself in war.[31]

On February 21, 1961, after several draft resolutions failed of adoption, the Council passed a resolution sponsored by the U.A.R., Ceylon, and Liberia. This resolution, adopted by a vote of 9-0-2, with Russia and France abstaining, was affirmed by the Assembly in April. It empowered ONUC to "take immediately all appropriate measures to prevent the occurrence of civil war in the Congo, including arrangements for cease-fires, the halting of all military operations, the prevention of clashes, and the use of force, if necessary in the last resort."[32] Other relevant provisions called for the evacuation of Belgian paramilitary and military personnel, political advisers, and mercenaries, and an impartial investigation into Lumumba's death. The Council also urged "the convening of Parliament and the taking of necessary protective measures in that connection."[33] ONUC now had legal approval for pressuring Tshombe

[31] Alexander Dallin, *The Soviet Union at the U.N.* (New York: Praeger, 1962), p. 150.
[32] Security Council Resolution S/4722, February 21, 1961.
[33] *Ibid.*, Part B, para. 1.

to remove Belgians from Katanga and for rendering assistance to Congolese political leaders or civilians threatened by the disorderly ANC.

The Secretary-General welcomed the new resolution as a clearer indication of the Council's attitude toward ONUC. Five countries, including the United States, stated that the type of force authorized in the operative paragraphs would not conflict with the Charter's prohibition in Article 2:7 and that force would not be employed to impose a political settlement. On its face the resolution seemed to accord with Hammarskjöld's previously stated views on the suitable relationship between ONUC's political and military functions:

> I reject everything that would have a touch of control or direction of the Congo's internal affairs . . . and, second, I do not believe that the use of military initiative, or pressure, is the way to bring about the political structure in terms of persons or institutions which is at present the first need of the Congo. The United Nations can help in such a direction, but that is by the normal political and diplomatic means of persuasion and advice, not by the use of force or intimidation.[34]

But eight months after independence, the remaining Congolese de jure and de facto authorities had shown themselves incapable of resolving their disputes by their own "normal political and diplomatic means." It was obvious that a new political structure could not be built without some form of international assistance. Authorization for active U.N. conciliation, avoided in the July

[34] General Assembly, *Official Records*, Fifteenth Session, 953rd Plenary Meeting (December 17, 1960), p. 1372, para. 182.

and August Council resolutions, had developed first in the Assembly's September resolution and later in the Council's February resolution. Clearly, rival national influences would be a factor in determining the type of political edifice U.N. organs and field representatives would labor to construct. The tone of the February resolution accented prevention; the Council did not specify what "measures" were to be taken to secure the withdrawal of Belgian military and political advisers and mercenaries. In February it was apparent that any use of force by ONUC would invite controversial interpretations from Congolese leaders and their foreign sponsors, who could easily challenge U.N. officials' definitions of the term "last resort." Council members were unable to agree on a resolution authorizing ONUC to use the necessary force to prevent atrocities against political leaders in the various Congolese cities.

The period from July 1960 to February 1961 had tested ONUC's capacity to maintain sufficient order to make the host state viable and to prevent unilateral interventions. The Soviet Union had been prevented from large-scale intrusion with men and supplies, chiefly due to Washington's insistence that the Sudan and Egypt forbid Russian over-flights of their territories. But in February 1961 the host state's government lacked both viability and constitutional authorization. With its old mandate unrealized, ONUC took on additional responsibilities with a markedly inadequate force-in-being.[35]

[35] India, Ethiopia, Malaya, Liberia, Nigeria, and Tunisia contributed new contingents to raise the troop level to 23,000—the bare minimum thought to be needed for effective policing of the Congo's six provinces. But numbers did not constitute the sole logistical problem ONUC faced in patrolling the huge African territory. While politically the participation of smaller countries was desirable, their unsophis-

ONUC's field representatives now undertook more intensive efforts to promote a political settlement in the Congo, while the Force's attempts to stabilize the country continued. These efforts were hampered by Tshombe's assertions of "self-determination" for Katanga and by his program to secure recognition from African and non-African states. Under its President's direction, Katanga displayed the trappings of statehood: officials issued coins, collected a gendarmerie, and retained revenues paid into the provisional treasury by its principal source of economic and political support, the Union Minière de Haut Katanga. The annual payment of $40 million in royalties and taxes by UMHK, a mining complex controlled by British and Belgian interests, enabled Tshombe to buy arms, pay mercenaries, and maintain an international propaganda machine hostile to the United Nations, the Central Government, and the United States. The extent of UMHK's influence was apparent to U.N. field representatives:

> It is possible to accept the statement that the Union Minière as such was not promoting, actively and directly, secessionist politics in Katanga. . . . But of

---

ticated military preparedness, lack of combat experience and command training, plus their lack of equipment—especially jet aircraft—meant that the Secretary-General had to look elsewhere for assistance. In 1961 alone, the U.S. Air Force flew 1,339 sorties, airlifted over 46,000 troops and 7,000 tons of supplies and gear for ONUC. Without advance planning it was inevitable that the lines of authority between U.N. civilian and military personnel required constant redefinition. Throughout the operation civilian control of ONUC was unquestioned, but military officials complained that their views on intelligence gathering and neutralization of the ANC did not receive a full hearing. For a discussion of other logistical-military problems the U.N. Force encountered in the Congo, see Edward Bowman and James Fanning, "Logistical Problems of UNEF and ONUC," *International Organization*, XVII (Spring 1963), 355-377.

course such "non-intervention" in the affairs of a State whose foundations the company had encouraged, if not instigated, a State which lived on duties paid to it by the company in defiance of the law of the Congo, and which was known to be defended on the international plane by the company's agents and money was non-intervention of a rather special kind.[36]

The efforts of the Organization to promote a political solution to the internal conflicts in the Congo were not limited to the activities of field officials. In November 1960 a U.N. Conciliation Commission was formed under the Advisory Committee's aegis as stipulated in the Assembly's resolution of September 20th. Amid the growing feeling of African leaders and Western statesmen that some form of legal government could and should be established, Nigeria's Jaja Wachuku led the Commission to the Congo and conducted interviews with major political figures there. After six weeks of observation in January and February 1961 the group could report no headway in reconciling differences, but agreement was reached on the conditions that should prevail if a constitutional government were to be restored. The Commission concluded that a government of national unity, a federal structure, was the only form of government that could preserve the independence and political integrity of the Congo. The Commission declared in its report of March 1961 that necessary steps toward attainment of national reconciliation should include the reconvening of parliament under proper protection, a summit conference of Congolese leaders, the drafting of a new constitution to replace the *Loi Fondamentale*, the

[36] O'Brien, *To Katanga and Back*, pp. 175ff.

evacuation of foreign political and military personnel, the release of political prisoners, and the reorganization of the army.[37] The Commission's recommendations were a catalogue of the Congo's political and military troubles, and they furnished Hammarskjöld with broadly based goals for conciliatory efforts, but these were goals suggested by outside observers. They reflected the aims of some, but not all, of the leaders interviewed in the field.

By the time the Conciliation Commission's report was made available, difficulties which continued to complicate the task of finding political solutions to the Congo's post-independence chaos had emerged. Outside parties —representatives of the United Nations or national statesmen (and later, delegations from the OAU)— could propose solutions to rival leaders in the Congo, but these political figures were under no obligation to accept offers of mediation or conciliation under the direction of any state or grouping of states. Yet they were susceptible to the influences of their foreign backers. Outside parties lost no time in making suggestions, but these plans for "national reconciliation," for a federal structure, often reflected a Western penchant for representative political institutions which in the perspective of the protracted strife in the Congo seem ill-suited to the indigenously African aspects of the Congo's politics—the palaver and the proliferation of loyalties to entities smaller than the state.[38]

The United Nations' first efforts at active conciliation in the field looking toward a resolution of disorder and a termination of secession took the form of encouraging

[37] See U.N. Doc. A/4711 and Add. 1 and 2, March 20, 1961.
[38] See Spiro, pp. 115-129.

rival Congolese leaders to convene. The Tananarive conference was attended by Kasavubu, Kalonji, Tshombe,
and Joseph Ileo. Each leader was eager to appear in a
dominant role in order to secure the most favorable
terms of settlement for himself and his interests. Tshombe dominated the proceedings, submitting a plan for a
new constitution based on the idea of a confederal
rather than a federal state structure. This idea was not
fully explored because on its face it seemed to weaken
the authority of the Central Government in favor of the
provinces, especially rich Katanga. The conference
yielded evidence that the palaver method of negotiation was being followed. In the interval between the
Tananarive conference and a second conference at Co-
quihatville, other patterns of political behavior peculiar
to non-Western modes of diplomacy began to trouble
U.N. personnel working closely with Congolese political figures to find a solution to the grave threats still
facing the strife-torn country. Leaders issued statements
featuring ultimata which were never acted upon; politicians praised and denounced the United Nations and
brother African leaders or rival Congolese authorities
with little regard for consistency.

In the interval between the two conferences, the
Leopoldville moderates who had endorsed a federal
structure reached a new agreement with ONUC. The
U.S. government had also expressed its support for a
federal arrangement, stressing that the unequal dis-
tribution of the Congo's economic resources made federal ties necessary for viability. Thus when the Congolese leaders reconvened, Tshombe found himself isolated. His subsequent arrest and detention when the
negotiations broke down dramatized the *opera comique*

quality of the entire conference and the immaturity of the negotiators. After intensive efforts on the part of U.N. field personnel, plans were drawn up for the re-convening of the Congolese Parliament under full U.N. protection. Tshombe, at first acceding to the session, dis-avowed his pledge once he returned to Elizabethville. The United Nations' elaborate precautions for the safe conduct of delegates and tight security regulations placed the Organization squarely behind the new pre-mier chosen to lead the Congo, Cyrille Adoula. The restoration of legal government in the formal sense con-tributed little to the solution of the underlying prob-lem of national reconciliation in the substantive sense. Yet the Adoula government was an administration bet-ter equipped to deal with the United Nations in its ef-forts to protect civilian personnel from attacks and to terminate the secession, especially in view of the U.S. strengthened support of the Leopoldville regime.

The new Central Government came into existence in August 1961 pledged to expel all mercenaries and for-eign officers serving in Katanga. The Adoula govern-ment's decree echoed the terms of the Council's Febru-ary resolution. A common design for Katanga's rein-tegration into a unitary Congo state had taken form. Behind the U.S. and U.N. concern for the Congo's po-litical structure, concern leading to the events of Sep-tember 1961, lay fears of impending economic collapse. Washington and New York officials were agreed that the Congo could survive as an economic unit only if Katanga's disproportionate wealth was redirected into Leopoldville coffers. Massive bilateral U.S. aid and the U.N. civilian operation could not shore up the tottering country permanently.

Restoration of a constitutional government in Leopoldville appeared to usher in a more promising period for U.N. attempts to maintain order, conciliate factional leaders, and stabilize the ANC. Tribal violence in Katanga between Tshombe's forces and the Balubas continued as a constant challenge to U.N. troops, whose role continued to be unclear after passage of the February 21st resolution. Despite Hammarskjöld's unlimited endorsement of the Adoula government and his agreement with the new Prime Minister that termination of Katanga's secession should receive the highest priority, the Secretary-General remained cautious in his interpretation of the February 21st resolution and the degree of force ONUC might use in achieving a common objective. For Hammarskjöld, the legal basis of ONUC's mandate remained unchanged by the Council's February resolution. He stood by an earlier judgment:

> Certainly the Council cannot be deemed to have instructed the Secretary-General, without stating so explicitly, to act beyond the scope of his own request or contrary to the specific limitation regarding nonintervention in internal conflicts which he stated to the Council. Moreover, in the light of the domestic jurisdiction limitation of the Charter, it must be assumed that the Council would not authorize the Secretary-General to intervene with armed troops in any internal conflict when the Council had not specifically adopted enforcement measures under Articles 41 and 42 of Chapter VII of the Charter.[39]

The absence of a specific Council authorization under Articles 41 and 42 left Article 40 to serve as a possible

[39] U.N. Doc. S/P.V. 887, July 20, 1960, p. 17.

legal basis for ONUC.[40] Although the Council failed to mention Article 40 explicitly in its resolutions on ONUC, Hammarskjöld shared the view that the article might be construed as the basis of authorization for the U.N. Force.[41] Such an authorization, he stressed, placed legal and practical limits on the Organization's capacity to intervene in the Congo's affairs, in view of Article 2:7.

The question of ONUC's mandate, especially its use of force, and the question of priorities for ONUC in carrying out Council directives, were posed with particular urgency in the months following August 1961, when, five months after passage of the February resolution, the Belgian officers and the South African and other mercenaries who had not been withdrawn pursuant to that resolution became the chief object of concern to the Leopoldville government and U.N. field representatives.[42]

[40] The majority of the International Court's judges upheld the generally accepted opinion that Article 42 had not served as the constitutional foundation for ONUC in an advisory opinion of July 1962, "Certain Expenses of the United Nations"; see *Yearbook of the International Court of Justice*, 1961-1962, pp. 78-84.

[41] See Oscar Schachter, "Preventing the Internationalization of Internal Conflict: A Legal Analysis of the U.N. Congo Experience," American Society of International Law *Proceedings*, 1963, pp. 219ff.

For a detailed discussion of the constitutional foundation of ONUC, and of U.N. Forces generally, see D. W. Bowett, *United Nations Forces* (New York: Praeger, 1964), pp. 174-183, 274-312.

[42] As Lefever observes, the preoccupation of U.N. officials with the objective of expelling Belgian military and political advisers from the Congo, especially Katanga, strained relations between the Secretariat and the Belgian government in the first ten months of ONUC's existence. On occasion Dayal and others failed "to discriminate between those Belgians who were prepared to play a constructive role in an independent Congo and to cooperate with the U.N. mandate, and those who were not so disposed." (*Crisis in the Congo*, p. 70.) Relations between the Secretariat and the Belgian government improved when Paul-Henri Spaak returned to the Belgian foreign ministry in March 1961, prior to the U.N. operations to be described.

A widely publicized incident in September 1961 dramatized the complications that occurred when Hammarskjöld's civilian representatives attempted to carry out field missions with military aspects. The U.N. command in Elizabethville planned "Operation Rumpunch" as a means of apprehending and evacuating mercenaries in Katanga. A bloodless undertaking, Rumpunch was partially successful; but after its completion 104 officers from a list drawn up by Katangese ministers for the U.N. representatives were missing. Conor Cruise O'Brien, who participated in the round-up, reports that the operation as a whole was marred by lack of intelligence analyses and lack of U.N. forces in strategic locations like Kolwezi and Jadotville. ONUC thus had difficulty monitoring the re-entry of foreign military or paramilitary officers into Katanga from Rhodesia and Angola. A second operation, Morthor, planned to clarify Rumpunch, was timed to be completed prior to Hammarskjöld's expected arrival in the Congo. Morthor did not proceed as U.N. field officials had anticipated. Fighting broke out, and press reports assailed the United Nations for its alleged initiative in the use of force. An eight-day clash was touched off by these events, events for which explanations are still controversial.[43]

Nevertheless, "The Secretariat's position on the Belgian question frightened away, at least for a time, an undetermined number of Belgian specialists and thus had the unintended effect of denying the Congo desperately needed assistance in every sector of economic, civil, and military life. This may have delayed recovery in some areas by years. Technicians recruited by the United Nations from other countries made a significant contribution, but in terms of quantity or quality they were not equal to the Belgians they replaced." (*Ibid.*)

[43] For a detailed discussion of the fighting, see Lefever, *Crisis in the Congo,* pp. 79-88; Arthur Lee Burns and Nina Heathcote, *Peacekeeping by U.N. Forces, From Suez Through the Congo* (New York:

O'Brien writes that Morthor had been planned as an operation to end Katanga's secession, that the U.N. authorities in Leopoldville approved the operation, which in order to be successful would include the arrest of certain Katangan officials and the occupation by the United Nations of key gendarmerie headquarters.[44] According to O'Brien, when the press, the British government, and others questioned the use of force by ONUC, the Secretary-General might have flown to Elizabethville, obtained a cease-fire, and then dismissed all three field representatives involved in Morthor for exceeding their instructions; or, if the Secretary-General had wanted to cover for Khiary and O'Brien, he might have justified Morthor as a legitimate action under the February resolution authorizing the use of force to prevent civil war; or, he asserts, Hammarskjöld might have labelled Katanga the cause of internal conflict and defended Morthor as an attempt to install the legitimate Congo government in Elizabethville on grounds that the February resolution had superseded paragraph 4 of the August 9th resolution. Not surprisingly, the Secretary-General chose another course, one in keeping with his own precepts and his awareness of the shifting political majority behind the February 1961 resolution as opposed to those of 1960. After consultation with his closest advisers in Leopoldville and New York (all of whom denied knowledge of instructions to undertake an operation aimed at ending the secession), Hammarskjöld issued a public statement in which he stressed that Morthor was to be interpreted as a continuation

---

Praeger, 1963), pp. 100-131; O'Brien, *To Katanga and Back*, pp. 63-330.

[44] O'Brien, *To Katanga and Back*, pp. 240ff.

of Rumpunch and the United Nations' use of force as "defensive."[45]

The first military engagement between ONUC and the Katangese gendarmerie ended in embarrassment for the United Nations and a cease-fire agreement denigrated by both the Soviet Union and Central Government officials, who regarded it as a capitulation to the rebel leader. Hammarskjöld's death, coupled with the incomplete evacuation of mercenaries and continued violence after the September fighting, resulted in greater U.S. and Secretariat impatience with Tshombe's quixotic behavior, impatience increased by the lack of compliance with the provisional cease-fire order of September 20th. By November 1961 the political majority behind the February resolution had shifted. Russia now favored the use of force by the United Nations to apprehend the remaining foreign mercenaries, as did the United States. But the British government concurred with the French government, whose representative insisted that "the use of force may have the opposite results to those intended by the Council."[46] Over the protests of the two European states, the United States led the Council to passage of a new resolution deepening the Organization's commitment to the Central Government.

The November 24th resolution authorized the Acting Secretary-General, U Thant,

> to take vigorous action, including the use of requisite measure of force, if necessary, for the immediate ap-

[45] U.N. Doc. S/4940, September 14, 1961, p. 103.

[46] Security Council, *Official Records*, Sixteenth Year, 982nd Meeting (November 24, 1961), para. 60. See also, 976th Meeting (November 17, 1961), paras. 157, 164, 166-169.

prehension, detention pending legal action and/or deportation of all foreign military and paramilitary personnel and political advisers not under the United Nations Command, and mercenaries as laid down in paragraph A-2 of the Security Council resolution of February 21, 1961.[47]

The resolution also requested Thant "to take all necessary measures to prevent the entry or return of such elements under whatever guise and also of arms, equipment or other material in support of such activities." The Council also declared that "all secessionist activities against the Republic of the Congo are contrary to the *Loi fondamentale* and Security Council decisions and specifically *demands* that such activities which are now taking place in Katanga shall cease forthwith."

The Council's resolution of November 24, 1961, did not refer to Articles 41 or 42 in keeping with the convictions members (except the Soviet Union) had expressed, in the first four resolutions and in debates preceding their adoption, that ONUC should not be construed as enforcement action against any state or interested party. The firm U.S. position plus the Belgian Foreign Minister Spaak's endeavors to bring Adoula and Tshombe together permitted Thant to counter British and French opposition to the November 24th resolution with a pledge to press for national reconciliation. Thant showed that he had different ideas, or perhaps a different style from that of his predecessor, in the conduct of the United Nations' second military operation against the rebel province.

On November 30th, Sture Linner reported from Eliza-

---

[47] Security Council Resolution S/5002, November 24, 1961.

bethville that increased tension and attacks on U.N. officials demonstrated Tshombe's inability to control his forces or to alter his policies toward the United Nations and its resolutions. Linner's fears of new hostilities materialized in December. The action taken by ONUC occurred before the political majority behind the November resolution could disintegrate. Although the operation involved offensive tactics and 6,000 men as compared with 1,400 employed in the September encounters, the second military action was described by U.N. officials as "defensive," as an attempt to "regain and assure our freedom of movement, to restore law and order . . . and to react vigorously in self-defense to every assault on our present positions."[48] As fighting spread, numerous governments pressed for a cease-fire.

What emerged from the United Nations' second military action in Katanga was closer cooperation between U.S. authorities and ONUC's executive directors. The American role in seeking a political solution grew more obvious, as the American ambassador, in close touch with Washington, arranged a Tshombe-Adoula meeting and secured the adherence of the two leaders to the eight-point Kitona Declaration, a document affirming the *Loi Fondamentale* and the unity of the Congo under Kasavubu's control. The British and Belgian interests in Katanga helped Tshombe in his dilatory attitude toward his Kitona pledges. For six months, U.N. field representatives, operating under vague mandates, confined their role to passive good offices, providing safe conduct for delegates to conferences, and attempting to create a favorable atmosphere for negotiations between the secessionist groups and the Central Government. Sporadic

[48] U.N. Doc. S/5025, December 15, 1961, p. 14.

talks led to acceptance of U.N. proposals in the military, monetary, transport, and communications field, but the future relationship of Katanga to the Republic remained unsettled, as rival political leaders blamed each other for delays.

In keeping with their earlier attitudes toward the secession, the United States and Secretariat officials continued to press for a solution favorable to the Leopoldville government's interests. The submission of the Thant Plan for National Reconciliation in August 1962 marked the beginning of a new, more active phase in peaceful settlement attempts. The Thant Plan was put forward as a non-negotiable proposal, to be accepted or rejected by the parties in its entirety. Its provisions called for adoption of a new federal constitution to be drafted by a special U.N. commission, an interim division of Katanga's revenues from taxes, mining concessions, royalties, and other sources on a fifty-fifty basis with the Central Government, termination of the secession, currency reunification, a general amnesty, and revision of the Leopoldville administration to include representatives of all political parties and all provinces.[49] The Plan provided for the consideration of economic sanctions if Tshombe did not indicate a willingness to comply with its stipulations.

Continued unrest in the Congo stimulated Thant to ask members, in December 1962, to consider the applicability of economic sanctions to force Tshombe's cooperation. The diverging attitudes of the European states, with economic interests in Katanga, and the United States, with interests in working out federal solutions using the United Nations, blocked realization

49 U.N. Doc. S/5053, Add. 11, August 20, 1962, pp. 16-17.

of the sanctions idea. The U.S.-backed Adoula government quickly accepted the Thant Plan (of which the American government was the principal architect), while Tshombe first accepted, then procrastinated. In a short-lived attempt to placate Britain and Belgium, the United States submitted and then hastily withdrew the McGhee Plan, which would have allowed Katanga a greater share in revenues and more autonomy vis-à-vis the Central Government than the Thant Plan. The Thant Plan, submitted to the parties as an externally sponsored solution, committed the prestige of the United Nations to a particular set of recommendations and to the fortunes of a demonstrably insecure if legal central regime. Technically, parties were not obligated to accept federalism as the final solution, but the pressures brought to bear on the various parties bilaterally and via ONUC were strong. The Organization, in promoting a federal rather than a confederal structure, sought to avoid the extremes of Balkanization in Africa and the repressiveness of a unitary state composed of hostile sub-groups. In theory, such a solution appeared sound; but in practice, the inability of a central regime in Leopoldville to exert its authority throughout the state indicated that a federal solution could be achieved only if imposed by an outside party, by the United States–United Nations. In terms of the Congo's long-range future, such an outside settlement might prove unacceptable to provincial groups within the country and to other African states, in similar post-colonial political straits, who feared "neo-imperialism."

A year of active U.S.–U.N. involvement in promoting direct but unsuccessful negotiations between Congo disputants and a joint effort against the Orientale gendarmerie supporting Gizenga drew to a close in December 1962 with Tshombe's failure to comply with the Thant Plan. The United States and the Soviets were now in agreement to use force against Katanga via ONUC, but for different reasons. In the face of continued provocative attacks against ONUC, the Secretary-General pressed for logistical support from the United States sufficient to terminate the secession militarily. As a result of General Lewis Truman's mission to the Congo, the United States supplied Thant with new aircraft, radio communications, and truck transports needed to carry out a third military action in Katanga. The fact that resistance from an estimated 20,000 mercenaries fell away, permitting the United Nations to take over the province, made the operation seem less contentious than it might have been in view of Tshombe's announced intention to pursue a scorched earth policy in the province rather than yield. Defending the action as a step needed to ensure ONUC's "freedom of movement," a purpose for which the Council had not authorized the use of force in specific resolutions, Thant later placed the military actions in Katanga in a different light: "Other than its successful efforts to eliminate the mercenaries in South Katanga, in pursuance of the Security Council mandate, the Force took no military initiatives involving the use of force; it launched no offensive."[50]

The success of the third military action was marred by a series of events in early January 1963. A brief pause

[50] U.N. Doc. S/5784, June 29, 1964, p. 40. "Freedom of movement" had been the subject of discussion between U.N. officials and Congolese authorities from the beginning of the field mission. Guarantees were written into the original agreement between the Leopoldville leaders and the Organization.

in the United Nations' third military action in Katanga was followed on December 30th by an announcement from Robert A. Gardiner, the U.N. operations chief in Leopoldville, that the U.N. forces were "not going to make the mistake this time of stopping short." "This is going to be as decisive as we can make it," Gardiner was quoted as saying.[51] On January 1, ONUC troops entered Jadotville, an important center of operations for UMHK, apparently ignoring an order from Thant to refrain from entering the town. Ralph Bunche, sent to investigate what U.N. officials described as a "serious breakdown in communications and co-ordination,"[52] concluded that a recurrence of the Jadotville episode could be avoided by better liaison and a thorough overhaul of U.N. civil-military relations.[53] To some observers, "bad communications" seemed a euphemism for differences of opinion within the Secretariat command chain over the military action.[54]

ONUC's third and decisive military action in December 1962–January 1963 ended Katanga's secession; interested outside parties and the United Nations again turned to the political and economic problems of reintegrating the province into the Republic. The end of the secession was accomplished by the use of requisite force rather than by economic pressures or diplomatic means, but the issue of self-determination for all parts of the Congo appeared settled. With the endorsement of the left and center groups in the Assembly plus the Latin American states, the United States had won ap-

[51] *The New York Times,* January 1, 1963.

[52] U.N. Press Release, SG/1406, January 3, 1963.

[53] U.N. Doc. S/5053, Add. 14, January 10, 1963, pp. 156ff.

[54] See for example, Philip Ben, "Lessons of the Congo," The *New Republic,* January 26, 1963, pp. 7-8.

proval for the military operation; with the support of the right and center groups, the United States received backing for its decision to maintain Tshombe as a political force in the Congo. But the quest for a lasting political solution to the territory's disorders was impeded by the political vacuum in Katanga after Tshombe's flight from Elizabethville. While the end of Katanga's secession in itself eased the situation in the Congo, it threw the remaining political problems of the Republic into sharper relief. The Congo's future as an independent state, capable of coping with economic and internal security demands, appeared to depend upon whether massive aid along the lines urged by the American-sponsored Cleveland mission could prevent a further breakdown.

The future use of U.N. or other military forces in the Congo remained an unsolved issue in early 1963. The heavy financial and political burdens placed on the United Nations by a continuation of the field operation required that member-states reassess the status of ONUC. In February 1963 civil war seemed to have been averted. The Security Council, in its various resolutions, had empowered ONUC (1) to maintain the territorial integrity and political independence of the Congo; (2) to assist the Congo government in restoring and maintaining law and order; (3) to prevent the occurrence of civil war in the Congo; (4) to secure the immediate withdrawal and evacuation from the Congo of all foreign military and paramilitary personnel and all mercenaries; and (5) to render technical assistance. In February 1963 Thant reported that civil war had been prevented and that foreign military personnel had withdrawn, but that the Congo required additional technical assistance in the retraining of its disorganized army. Moreover, the Secretary-General warned, the country's precarious state of law and order could invite external interventions threatening the territorial integrity and political independence of the Congo Republic.[55] The Secretary-General envisioned a "caretaker" role for ONUC in a transition period to last until the termination of the Force's mandate.

As the question of terminating ONUC became less theoretical, member-states had to consider the alternatives open to the Organization in the light of information available. Should it continue to shoulder the burden that had threatened to topple the entire Organization? Could it pull out without additional damage to its prestige and finances, leaving the country to face an uncertain future, or take on the still heavier task of reconstruction for which it might be unequipped? The first Council resolution had left the question of termination indefinite; assistance to the Congo government would be rendered until the national security forces could perform their duties. Could the host state determine when the U.N. Force should cease to operate in its territory if a political majority in the Organization should feel that the situation constituted a threat to international peace and security? Could the host negotiate for ONUC's withdrawal or could the Force withdraw without the host state's acquiescence?

Although the ending of Katanga's secession produced a lessening of international concern for the Congo's future among those states whose primary interest in Belgian withdrawal had been satisfied, the American government persuaded Thant to accept a continuation of

[55] U.N. Doc. S/5240, February 4, 1963, pp. 98-99.

a reduced U.N. Force for at least six months.[56] After Thant confirmed December 31, 1963, as the deadline for the Central Government to assume responsibilities for law and order throughout the Congo, the Assembly voted sufficient funds to extend ONUC's life until June 30, 1964. The vote to extend ONUC represented a compromise between the more militant African states— Ghana and the U.A.R.—who felt the United Nations should withdraw, and the United States and other Western states, who feared a collapse of governmental authority and renewed tribal fighting. In yet another ad hoc financial improvisation, the United States and Britain agreed to pay the additional $10 or $12 million needed to maintain 3,000 troops in the Congo for another six months.

Between January and June 1964 the phasing out of ONUC continued. In advance of ONUC's departure, the United Nations and the Adoula government failed to conclude agreements for the reorganization of the army. Revolts in Kivu dramatized the obvious fact that the poorly trained, inefficient 35,000-man army would not be able to meet the internal security requirements of the country after ONUC's termination. Plans for Canada, Norway, Israel, and others to take on responsibility for individual segments of the ANC also faltered. Although proposals for Nigerian or other African forces to render military assistance never came to fruition, the Congo government did not request an extension of ONUC beyond the June deadline.

As ONUC prepared to withdraw in mid-1964, efforts to seal Katanga's reintegration into the Republic with a new draft constitution resulted in the passage of a

[56] Lefever, *Crisis in the Congo*, p. 133.

document emulating the French Fifth Republic's provisions. The Adoula regime, heavily dependent on U.S. diplomatic, economic, and other support, had failed to reconcile the political differences which continued to divide the country four years after independence. The new presidential system indicated that Congolese legislators had little difficulty in establishing some of the forms of a representative governmental structure, but the substance, the underlying consensus needed to make such a system work, was lacking. Amid spreading rebellion in Kivu and other sections, Tshombe emerged from a palaver of the provincial authorities left in the Congo as the head of an interim government dubbed "Government of National Reconciliation." As the new administration took control, it was clear that reconciliation expressed a hope, not a reality. With the exception of Kalonji, no other regional figure of consequence was included in the Cabinet. The open hostility of other African states to Tshombe's new role suggested that the Congo's troubles were far from over.

The United Nations' official responsibilities for political solutions, for dealing with secessionist movements, and for protecting human rights in the Congo ended with ONUC's departure. The U.S. involvement continued as the Tshombe government relied on American and Belgian assistance in putting down challenges to central authority. The new Tshombe administration faced the need to reform the corrupt provincial administrations, to restore order, and to staff the Leopoldville government, enormous tasks in view of the elections promised after a four-year hiatus. Six months later, despite the presence of U.S. planes, white mercenary troops and Cuban exile pilots and military instructors, the legally constituted Tshombe government in Leopoldville had not succeeded in quelling rebellions that threatened to bring down the Central regime. The U.S.-Belgian airlift in November 1964 further demonstrated the security problems of the vast territory. The widespread political repercussions of the rescue mission pointed up a crucial aspect of the Congo's post-ONUC confusion: as the "white man's puppet" who led the secession of Katanga province, Tshombe was vilified to the point where no military aid could be expected to come from other African nations even if the former rebel leader had agreed to broaden the base of his "Government of National Reconciliation."

Similarly, expectations that the Organization of African Unity might play a constructive role in the transition period after ONUC's termination were dashed by reactions of individual African leaders to the continuing rebellion against Tshombe's central government and the Belgian-American rescue mission. The increasing radicalism of the governments of Ghana, the U.A.R., and Algeria[57] led Nigeria's Jaja Wachuku to charge, in December 1964, that the Congo's difficulties stemmed from "the refusal of certain African states to accept the basic fact that the Congo is a sovereign state."[58] Objecting to Tshombe's "neo-colonialist" orientation, the militant African leaders minimized the massacre of white hostages in Stanleyville and played up the "imperialist intervention" and the "massacres" of Congolese by mercenaries when the Council discussed the November 1964 Belgian-American airlift. The likelihood of additional Belgian-American "interventions" in the Congo was

[57] See Colin Legum, "What Kind of Radicalism for Africa," *Foreign Affairs*, XLIII (January 1965), 237-251.
[58] The *New York Times*, December 6, 1964.

diminished by the outcry (largely racially tinged) from smaller states in the Council meetings of December.[59] Nevertheless, the facade of African unity was laid bare in the vituperative Council debates on the Belgian-American operation. Prior to the rescue mission, the OAU's Conciliation Commission failed in its attempts to negotiate the release of rebel-held prisoners, revealing the impotence of the regional body. Fissures within the membership of the OAU, with some states intervening in behalf of the rebels and some arguing for recognition of the legitimacy of the Tshombe government, cast doubt on the possibility of a constructive role for the OAU in the remaining issues of peaceful change affecting Africa.

From the standpoint of the Organization's experience in internal disorders, ONUC will remain highly significant in view of the scale and duration of the United Nations' effort. The preceding discussion has emphasized that events quickly demonstrated the inadequacy of Hammarskjöld's conceptions for the United Nations' actions in the Congo, conceptions derived from previous experiences in Lebanon and Suez. Central to the late Secretary-General's thinking was the deeply rooted conviction that the United Nations via ONUC should neither become a party to internal conflicts nor influence their outcome. This conviction could provide operational guidance for field officials only if outside powers refrained from endorsing or aiding any rival local authorities and if the host government maintained sufficient control over the country's economic, political, and

[59] See Security Council, *Official Records*, Nineteenth Year, 1170th-1173rd Meetings, 1175th-1178th Meetings, 1181st and 1183rd-1189th Meetings (December 9, 10, 15-30, 1964).

military life. But if a central government had control over these areas there would be no need for U.N. or other interventions or interpositionary corps. The tendency of the Council's permanent members to aid factional leaders invalidated one of Hammarskjöld's assumptions; the continuing constitutional crisis invalidated the other.

By playing up Belgian interference in the Congo rather than the Congo's internal political problems, Hammarskjöld and Congolese leaders established an order of priorities relegating conciliation to a secondary place during ONUC's early stages. Later when Hammarskjöld (leaning heavily on American political initiatives as well as funds) did back the Adoula government against Katanga, the unstable political majorities in the Council and Assembly favoring strengthened directives for ONUC crippled the United Nations in its dealings with Tshombe, who relied on British and Belgian economic interests to support the continued secession. Abstentions and negative votes on Council resolutions were a sign that Hammarskjöld's position was becoming increasingly untenable.

The long peace-keeping effort in the Congo placed extensive responsibilities on the Secretary-General's office. The experience gained in interpreting mandates and managing a complicated field operation established a reservoir of information applicable to future internal conflicts. But just as the financial reserves of the United Nations alone were inadequate for the Congo's needs, so too the techniques of the multilateral organization alone proved insufficient to achieve what now appears to be the too ambitious goal of national reconciliation. Grave problems developed from the expectation that

ONUC could be involved in both negative and positive political and military tasks at the same time. If the Organization's negative task of preventing the escalation of local conflicts and establishing law and order were difficult to accomplish, the task of fostering national reconciliation along lines prescribed by Western states proved equally difficult. Efforts to initiate negotiations among Congolese officials were left to field personnel, who, equipped with the Secretary-General's interpretations of Council and Assembly mandates, necessarily improvised when legalistic details of resolutions failed to fit the facts of the increasingly fluid situation in Elizabethville and other outlying cities. The Congolese parties to the series of internal conflicts were incapable of resolving their own differences along Western lines of political accommodation, yet capable of sabotaging any settlement put forward by the United Nations or others, much in the same way their foreign supporters were capable of undermining Council or Assembly resolutions. The need to collaborate with the United States for logistical and other military support for ONUC linked the Organization to American proposals for political solutions and exposed the Secretariat to hostile criticism from the excluded Soviet bloc.

While the United Nations' political and financial over-commitment in the Congo internal conflicts was most dramatically underlined by the controversy over the military operations conducted in Katanga, in the realm of political solutions the Organization's activities in the Congo also bore signs of over-extension. The prolonged effort to foster a political solution couched in terms of a federal structure and national reconciliation exemplifies the inherent difficulties in placing the burden for selecting or implementing such settlements on the Organization. Disorders in the Congo while ONUC was deployed and the unrest since the Force's withdrawal raise questions about the capacity of an international organization to find criteria for emerging countries without political traditions linked to statehood. The inapplicability of Western federalism or parliamentary rule to the Congo's political structure is apparent. Political institutions rooted in cultural traditions with a long history cannot be grafted onto a wholly different base.

In his final report on ONUC, Thant emphasized the weaknesses which had marked the four-year peace-keeping operation. Among the weaknesses he noted was the lack of integration of national units under a U.N. Command, a factor which hampered morale and effectiveness. Of far greater consequence for future peace-keeping operations was Thant's assessment of the Congo's future. In terms applicable to other internal disorders, he remarked,

I believe that a further extension of the stay of the Force in the Congo would provide no solution to the remaining problems of the Congo. The current difficulties in the country reflect conflicts of an internal political nature, with their main origins found in the absence of a genuine and sufficiently wide-spread sense of national unity among the various ethnic groups composing the population of the Congo. There is little assistance that the United Nations Force can render in that kind of situation since the solution of conflict depends entirely on the willingness and readiness of the Congolese political leaders and the traditional chiefs and their respective followers to merge their factional interests in a true effort toward national conciliation.[60]

Less than a year after ONUC's departure, its stay in the Congo appeared to have contributed to an interval, at best a hiatus, in the continuing local violence and range of external interventions by major powers and revolutionary African states determined to establish in the Congo a government to their ideological and political liking. This judgment was borne out by the attitudes interested parties adopted toward the Council's sixth resolution urging an end of all foreign intervention, a cease-fire, and withdrawal of foreign mercenaries.[61] The Council's resolution of December 30, 1964, marked a compromise between the demands of militant African states for condemnation of the U.S.–Belgian airlift and American interests in exposing the interference of others in the Congo's affairs. The ineffectuality of the resolution, which also called for the Organization of African Unity to promote efforts toward national reconciliation, became apparent as each group of interested parties announced its own interpretation. The United States argued that its military aid to Tshombe could not be considered "intervention" because it was sent at the request of the legitimate government. The radical African countries, Algeria, Ghana, and the U.A.R., defended their arms shipments to the rebels on grounds that as Africans they could not be considered "outsiders." And the Kasavubu-Tshombe incumbent government took the view that the cease-fire would permit the rebels to gather strength and would partition the Congo. The

[60] U.N. Doc. S/5784, June 29, 1964, p. 42.
[61] Security Council Resolution S/6129, December 30, 1964.

group of more moderate African states, including Nigeria and the Ivory Coast, while supporting the U.S. view on the legal aspects of intervention, decried the airlift and the use of white mercenaries by Tshombe.

The precarious stability the Congo enjoyed under the Kasavubu-Tshombe regime could not obscure the fact that behind a juridical facade of federal government, the Congo remained linked to competitive outside powers determined to influence its political complexion. The Congo's future, as regards a resumption of violence, is uncertain despite the extensive U.N. field mission. General Mobutu's military coup, his proclamation of a five-year presidency, and the subsequent challenges to his authority are evidence of continued political instability. Yet an assessment of ONUC's value to the Organization and to those states concerned with enhancing the contribution the United Nations might make in other internal disorders involving a breakdown of law and order must take into account the extent to which ONUC served the needs of the international society during its four-year history.

ONUC was able to function for a four-year period, although various states withdrew their troops, refused to pay assessments, or exerted bilateral pressures on the Secretary-General, field officials, and local political figures for political reasons. Although the Central Government in its successive forms argued with field personnel, no demands for ONUC's departure were issued. In fact, Russian and other moves to terminate ONUC abruptly were resisted. The conclusion emerges, as Ernest Lefever argues, that the operation served the interests of states concerned with a stable Africa, notably the United States, other Western nations, and the moderate African countries.[62] The operation did not serve the interests of states whose principal aim was to promote instability as a means of increasing national influence in the Congo—the Soviet Union, China, and the more radical African countries. Most important was the extent to which the operation served the larger international interest in peace, an interest that American, Soviet, or Belgian unilateral interventions might have failed to achieve had such interventions been attempted in the confused days of July 1960 or thereafter.

Cyprus

Like the breakdown of law and order in the Congo, the protracted internal conflict in Cyprus originated in tensions between communities. The internal disorder in Cyprus has embroiled the United Nations in disputes over treaty arrangements and guarantees for minority rights—questions the Organization had avoided in its previous involvement in internal conflicts. The Organization's treatment of the Cyprus question, in its political aspects as in its military aspects, indicates that member-states and Secretariat officials have tried to apply lessons derived from the Congo experience; but, unlike the Congo conflict, whose dimensions unfolded after the United Nations had become the "sole prop and hope" of the country,[63] the Cyprus conflict was fully matured and highly publicized when the Security Council considered the issue in March 1964. The Cyprus conflict, with international as well as internal aspects, returned to the Organization after a lapse of five years during which a settlement worked out by local parties in con-

[62] Lefever, *Crisis in the Congo*, p. 180.
[63] U.N. Doc. S/5784, June 29, 1964, p. 40.

junction with outside powers broke down and intensive conciliation efforts in a bilateral and regional framework failed to produce a solution. In view of the difficulties encountered in the Congo disorders, the Secretary-General and member-states were eager to avoid entangling the Organization in the Cyprus affair, as the discussion of the financing and time limits for UNFICYP will show; but in deciding to establish a new peace-keeping operation to cope with communal fighting that threatened international peace and security, the Council undertook to contain local violence and to prevent external interventions while working toward a political solution —goals similar to those pursued in the Congo conflict.

Historical, economic, geographical, and strategic considerations rather than abstract conceptions of self-determination figured prominently in the Zurich-London arrangements for Cyprus' transition from colonial rule to independence. Laborious negotiations among Britain, Greece, Turkey, and the two Cypriot groups yielded two treaties representing a compromise of interests. The Greek Cypriot demands for *enosis* with Greece, the Turkish Cypriot desires for ethnic partition, and British hopes of retaining the island as a military base were resolved in the Treaty of Guarantee and the Treaty of Alliance, both of which were incorporated in the island's constitution. The Treaty of Guarantee endorsed the territorial integrity and political independence of Cyprus and gave the three outside signatories the right to act singly or collectively to prevent annexation or partition. The Treaty of Alliance called for Cypriot-Greek-Turkish cooperation to defend the island against aggression and for British control of two military bases.

The outbreak of communal fighting in late December

1963 was touched off by President Makarios' announcement of thirteen proposals to alter the 1960 Constitution. These amendments were aimed at abolishing the requirement of majorities in both the Greek and Turkish Cypriot sides of the legislatures, so that tax laws and similar bills could be enacted. Other amendments called for the abolition of separate judicial systems for the two communities and separate municipal governments in the five major towns. The Archbishop's plans emphasized the need to eliminate the veto powers of the Turkish Cypriot Vice President. Turkish Cypriot leaders feared that these proposals would spell the end of protection of their rights as a minority. On January 1, 1964, Makarios stated his intention to seek abrogation of the treaties of alliance and guarantee,[64] confirming the suspicions of the minority that the constitutional amendments presaged a concerted campaign to change the island's political organization and external relations.

The vested interests of foreign powers in the future of the strife-torn Mediterranean island have created a heavily charged atmosphere in U.N. political councils. Each Cypriot community has a principal foreign sponsor, and Greece and Turkey are NATO members. British involvement stems from a treaty commitment and former colonial administration of the country, while American concerns since the conflict intensified have centered on averting war between Greece and Turkey and preventing Soviet manipulation of the Cypriot President, Archbishop Makarios. Since the eruption of violence on the island, the Cypriot communities and Greece and Turkey have attempted to employ a range of unilateral, bilateral, regional, and multilateral in-

[64] The *New York Times*, January 2, 1964.

strumentalities to ensure maximum gains with minimal concessions, short of uncontrolled hostilities.

The British government assumed the diplomatic and military lead in Cyprus from December 1963 to February 1964. British troops, constituting a small-scale peace-keeping force on the island, did not interpose themselves to prevent fighting between the warring factions, nor did they attempt to subdue or disarm irregular fighters. The British did manage to establish a truce zone in Nicosia, "the green line." Yet relations between British officers and local authorities were strained: a British official cautioned, "it is important that [a] United Nations force should not serve under the same rather humiliating terms of reference under which our men are now serving."[65]

Token U.N. participation in the present phase of the Cyprus civil war began in January 1964 with a British request, in association with Greece and Turkey, that U Thant station an observer on the island as his personal representative to monitor the cease-fire agreement between the Greek and Turkish Cypriots. Thant's cautious approach to this proposal indicated his desire to avoid a hasty involvement, especially in view of financial uncertainties. He replied that he would send a preliminary mission to Cyprus to ascertain whether the observer could play a useful role in maintaining the cease-fire.[66] But after objecting to the delay, British and other officials persuaded Thant to send General Gyani at once. Thant complied only after agreements had been reached on the terms of reference for the observer and arrangements had been concluded for Cyprus to pay the cost.[67]

[65] The *New York Times*, March 15, 1964.
[66] See U.N. Doc. S/5514, January 13, 1964.
[67] See U.N. Doc. S/5516, January 16, 1964.

Gyani's initial period of observation was set at six weeks and then extended for a second month while Thant consulted with interested parties. The Secretary-General, continuing his personal efforts to clarify the major issues and positions of all the parties concerned, underscored his careful approach in statements to the Council stressing that organ's authority to find a "reasonable and practical way out of what now appears to be an impasse," rather than his own.[68]

Thant's hesitation in taking on new responsibilities for the United Nations was understandable in view of previous "presences" or interventions in internal conflicts, notably those in Lebanon, Yemen, the Congo, and Laos. The public positions of Greece and Turkey and the two Cypriot communities toward the island's political future suggested that international mediation under U.N. or other auspices would be an arduous and uncertain process. Moreover, the complicated provisions of the treaties of alliance and guarantee would make a political solution to the Cyprus disorders more difficult to attain. But by February, pressures for U.N. commitment in the conflict had mounted, as efforts to promote an easing of tension and conciliation via NATO proved fruitless.

The British government's pre-conference round of talks between Duncan Sandys and Greek, Turkish, and Cypriot parties had indicated a willingness to parley, but in January it became clear that no party was willing to make the concessions necessary to transform the uneasy cease-fire into a permanent settlement. When the London conference ended in failure, the British, with

[68] Security Council, *Official Records*, Nineteenth Year, 1097th Meeting (February 25, 1964), para. 7.

American support, submitted a proposal for a three-month NATO-recruited peace-keeping force of 10,000 men to be under British command with political guidance from a committee of ambassadors. The plan called for the appointment of a mediator from a North Atlantic, non-NATO country to bring about a political solution. Behind-the-scenes negotiations resulted in Turkey's reluctant assent, Greek acceptance with some reservations, and Greek Cypriot rejection. Washington's agreement to co-sponsor the plan with Britain was subject to Cypriot approval for temporary suspension of the two contested treaties and avoidance of any Security Council control. The U.S. government was anxious to prevent Soviet intrusion into the affair via Council vetoes. Makarios demanded that the proposed force be made responsible to the Council, that Turkish troops be excluded and that mediation be confined to Britain, Greece, and Turkey, without the participation of the Turkish Cypriot minority. In a second counterproposal, the Archbishop expressed a preference for a Commonwealth rather than a NATO force. The unsuccessful London conference left unsettled questions of the mandate of the proposed force, the position of Greek and Turkish troops on the island, and the role of the United Nations.

When the United States assumed the initiative in February, State Department officials were eager to avoid seeming to favor either Greece or Turkey. Yielding to Greek Cypriot objections to the original U.S.–British peace-force proposal, the Americans agreed to "link" the force to the United Nations via "reports." They also agreed to eliminate Greek and Turkish participation, to include a Cyprus government official on the political committee advising the British commander, and to drop references to NATO in describing the force's composition. While American officials conferred with Makarios, and British officials with Thant, it became evident that the United States had perforce shifted its earlier attitude toward Security Council involvement. Recalling the Soviet Union's objections to dispatch of the Yemen Observation Mission until the Security Council gave its specific authorization, U.S. policy-makers were less adamant about excluding the Council entirely.

Revised U.S. proposals called for a "consensus" among Council members rather than a formal meeting and specific directives. When the amended plans still failed to win approval from Makarios, the United States had no choice but to go along with the separate decisions of Britain and Cyprus to request a Council meeting. Nevertheless, speculation on alternatives to the course adopted are worth pondering. Could the U.S. and British negotiators have given Makarios a choice of a NATO force or no force at all and risked Soviet intervention in the Cyprus dispute? Would Makarios have invited the Soviets to intervene directly and would they have done so? Could the two Western powers have arranged to have the Council meet in order to authorize a force whose composition and instructions were agreed upon in advance by the parties? The Archbishop's refusal to accept a regional peace-making force or continuation of the British force on Cyprus marked a defeat for Anglo-American diplomacy. It was clear that the Cypriot President's rejection did not derive from the military deficiencies of these proposals but from his conviction that the United Nations would serve as the most reliable mechanism for realization of his internal political goals. Controlling 80 percent of the island's population, the Archbishop has defined the problem as one of "self-determination" in an attempt to court the sympathies of the new states, who may be expected to support anti-colonialist positions in the General Assembly.

Daily postponements in Council meetings scheduled to debate the Cyprus question in late February attested to Thant's difficulties in securing agreement on a draft resolution. The Secretary-General sought a compromise formula that would take into consideration the Cypriot government's demand for Council endorsement of its territorial integrity and political independence without mention of the disputed treaties, and Turkey's demand for approval of the Constitution and the treaties. After a ten-meeting debate gave all parties, including the Turkish Cypriot representative, a chance to ventilate familiar charges and countercharges,[69] the Council unanimously endorsed a joint resolution submitted by the five non-permanent members, Bolivia, Norway, Morocco, the Ivory Coast, and Brazil. The eight-point resolution recommended the creation of a U.N. peace-keeping force with the consent of the Cyprus government, its size and composition to be determined by the Secretary-General in consultation with the governments of Britain, Turkey, Greece, and Cyprus.[70] Thant was instructed to appoint the commander of the Force, who would report to him on its operation. The Force was authorized to function for three months only, with all costs to be borne by the participating governments, in agreement with the Cyprus government, and supplementary funds to be donated on a voluntary

[69] See Security Council, *Official Records*, Nineteenth Year, 1094th–1102nd Meetings (February 7–March 4, 1964).

[70] Security Council Resolution S/5735, March 4, 1964.

basis.[71] The resolution further recommended that the Secretary-General designate a mediator, in agreement with the four parties, for the purpose of "promoting a peaceful solution and an agreed settlement of the problem confronting Cyprus, in accordance with the Charter of the U.N., having in mind the well-being of the people of Cyprus as a whole and the preservation of international peace and security."[72]

The first and confirming resolutions[73] on the Cyprus question indicated that the Council wished to avoid specific hazards experienced in the Congo. The clear separation between the functions of the U.N. Force and those of the U.N. mediator demonstrated the sentiments of member-states for a type of U.N. participation that would place the burden for resolving the issues of self-determination and human rights on the parties themselves rather than upon the Organization. Yet before a U.N. mediator acceptable to all parties could be selected, it was apparent that bilateral and regional conciliatory efforts would continue, regardless of prior failures and the parties' announced intentions to abide by the U.N. mediator's recommendations.

In the interim between July 1960 and March 1964 a plethora of suggestions for placing financial aspects of U.N. peace-keeping on a sounder basis and for establishing stand-by forces with available contingents and advance planning were put forward by individuals and governments. The Organization had not acted on any of these proposals, yet the difficulties it had faced in the Congo had made repetition of that involvement undesirable. The Cyprus resolution invested responsibility

[71] *Ibid.*, para. 6.   [72] *Ibid.*, para. 7.
[73] Security Council Resolution S/5603, March 13, 1964.

for the new Force in the Secretary-General. Russia, France, and Czechoslovakia dissented from that part of the resolution, in keeping with their attitudes toward the Congo operation. The same countries were equally disturbed by the instructions for the Cyprus Force, especially those on the use of force, yet they voted for the resolution, citing the Cyprus government's desire for it and the favorable arrangements for financing and termination. Despite the specific detail on the Force's composition, cost, and duration, the Council's resolution left the general mandate characteristically vague:

> ... the function of the Force should be, in the interest of preserving international peace and security, to use its best efforts to prevent a recurrence of fighting and, as necessary, to contribute to the maintenance and restoration of law and order and a return to normal conditions.[74]

In keeping with its general avoidance of specific citation of Charter articles in the resolutions on ONUC, the Council did not refer to any articles in Chapters VI or VII in its resolution establishing UNFICYP. Thant later described the Cyprus Force in terminology recalling that used by Hammarskjöld in discussing ONUC's constitutional foundation:

> This is not collective action against aggression undertaken under Chapter VII of the Charter.... It is something far more intricate and ... something of the greatest value, if it can succeed, as a precedent for the future. It is, in brief, an attempt on the international level to prepare the ground for the permanent, freely-agreed solution of a desperate and dangerous situa-

[74] *Ibid.*, para. 5.

tion by restoring peace and normality. The nature of this operation is far nearer to a preventive and protective police action; it is not repressive military action.[75]

The Council's separation of the Force's military functions from political tasks to be performed under the Secretary-General's aegis allowed Thant to recruit as his personal representatives in Cyprus individuals who were particularly suited to carry out these responsibilities. After the Force became operational, Thant tried to clarify the responsibilities of field officials still further by appointing a second mediator for day-to-day problems, so that the Force commander and the first mediator could concentrate on the Force's deployment and long-term political solutions respectively.

Problems of implementation of the Council's resolution arose immediately. While both Greek and Turkish spokesmen and their Cypriot counterparts expressed satisfaction with the compromise provisions, each side chose to interpret the Force's ambiguous mandate in terms favorable to itself. For Greece and Greek Cypriots, the resolution signified a U.N. commitment to prevent Turkish military intervention, while for Turkey and Turkish Cypriots, the injunction to "restore order" bound the U.N. Force to prevent Greek Cypriots from taking control of the whole island. Greek Cypriots believed that UNFICYP should help put down what it considered a domestic rebellion against the majority government. Turkish Cypriots, on the other hand, wanted the Force to stop the fighting and split the island into separate communities.

[75] U.N. Press Release, SG/SM/76, May 26, 1964, p. 5.

In implementing the Council's resolutions of March 4th and 13th, the Secretary-General faced two related problems: the technical establishment of the Force and the clarification of its mandate in the field. That the problems of recruitment and field conduct were linked was quickly shown in the poor response to Thant's request for contingents. In contrast to the initial willingness of states to contribute to ONUC, the Secretary-General encountered difficulties in persuading governments to participate in the Cyprus Force. Some were unwilling to pay; others feared that their troops might become engaged in combat with the large, heavily armed Greek Cypriot security forces and be asked to shoot civilians in order to restore calm. Recruitment was complicated also by Thant's pledge to take the wishes of the host state into account. Makarios' objection to inclusion of any U.S. or African troops narrowed the choice to Commonwealth countries, non-aligned states, and British troops already in Cyprus.

After ten days of strenuous negotiations, Thant received pledges from Canada, Ireland, Sweden, and Finland. UNFICYP had to be tailored to the needs of the specific conflict at hand, but the delay in establishing and fielding the Force pointed up the need for advance planning of peace-keeping operations. In a comparable situation, a country other than Turkey might have exercised its treaty right of intervention without waiting for recruitment problems to be resolved. UNFICYP became operational, in the Secretary-General's terms, twenty-three days after the initial Council resolution.[76] With

[76] Advance Canadian units were joined by additional troops from Austria, Denmark, New Zealand, and Australia. Donations of $1 million and $2 million from Britain and the United States respectively, plus medical supplies and air transport provided UNFICYP with the

the deployment of the Force in Cyprus, attention turned to instructions for UNFICYP's conduct in the field.

In outlining the new Force's terms of reference, Thant had to take into account the Turkish Cypriot community's insistent demands for guarantees of personal safety and the equally insistent demands of the Greek Cypriot community for assistance in restoring order throughout the entire island. Defining the terms of reference for UNFICYP thus involved delicate issues of U.N. relations with the host state, itself a party to the internal conflict. The British experience in peace-keeping in Cyprus convinced Thant that the U.N. Force must take a more active stance in preventing clashes between the two hostile Cypriot groups.

The Council's vague resolution left to Thant's discretion the precise ways in which UNFICYP would employ force, but another provision of the resolution made the Secretary-General's job of defining the permissible use of force for UNFICYP difficult. The government of Cyprus was called upon to exercise responsibility for the maintenance of law and order and "to take additional measures necessary to stop violence and bloodshed."[77] The Greek Cypriots therefore held that the U.N. troops should disarm the Turkish Cypriots. Thant argued that in so doing the Force would be interfering in the domestic affairs of Cyprus. The Secretary-General searched for a compromise formula that would satisfy the demands of interested parties and conform to the underlying principles of previous U.N. peace-keeping opera-

---

equipment to undertake its assignments. Continued hostilities on the island caused the estimates for a force of 3,000 to be revised upward to 10,000 and then drop back to 7,000.

[77] Security Council Resolution S/5735, March 4, 1964, para. 2.

tions, and that would avoid the pitfalls encountered in ONUC. Thant was not anxious to repeat the Morthor and Jadotville mishaps, nor was he eager to invite the type of invective that hampered ONUC when the late Secretary-General refused to place ONUC at Lumumba's disposal for subjugation of Katanga. Thant therefore instructed General Gyani that UNFICYP troops would be empowered to shoot in self-defense if engaged in interpositions between Turkish and Greek Cypriots.[78] These interpositions could be ordered by the Force Commander only, not by local commanders. Moreover, interposition would be authorized to enforce a prearranged cease-fire, if all parties agreed. The arrangements for a cease-fire would normally require UNFICYP to use persuasion rather than force. "Minimum force" could be ordered if either party threatened to "attack, envelop or infiltrate UNFICYP positions, thus jeopardizing the safety of troops in the area."[79] Thant's supplementary agreements with the Makarios government permitted the field commander to exercise his judgment in deciding whether to answer or disregard Greek Cypriot demands for help.

For the first month of its tour on Cyprus, the Force confined its activities to observation, patrol, and attempts to break up small clashes all over the island. A severe test of UNFICYP's instructions took place when Greek Cypriot forces launched a heavy attack on St. Hilarion castle, an ancient fortress serving as a Turkish Cypriot stronghold on the Kyrenia range. The violence and apparent premeditation of the attack contradicted earlier Greek Cypriot public statements that the Makarios government would not undertake military opera-

[78] See U.N. Doc. S/5653, April 11, 1964.　　[79] *Ibid.*

tions without informing UNFICYP. General Gyani, replying to Turkish Cypriot charges that the U.N. Force
should have intervened in the April battle, castigated
Greek Cypriot officials, with whom relations were already strained.[80] Despite UNFICYP's minor success in
disarming one band of Greek Cypriot irregulars, it was
evident that Thant's first instructions committed the
Force to a passive role that was ineffective in view of
the prevailing field situation.

Thant responded to the St. Hilarion episode by submitting an over-all peace plan designed to restore normal conditions to Cyprus.[81] The plan called for the two
Cypriot communities to disarm all civilians other than
the regular police, the gendarmerie, and the army.[82]
In addition, Thant asked for freedom of movement on
all Cyprus roads and in its towns, evacuation and removal of fortified positions beginning in Nicosia, rein-
tegration of Turkish Cypriots into their normal positions
in the police and other government services, arrangements for a general amnesty, and restoration of the normal functioning of the judiciary.[83] Thant appointed
Galo Plaza Lasso as a special representative to negotiate
short-term plans for preventing clashes, dismantling for-
tifications and roadblocks, disarming irregulars, controlling extremists, and reintegrating Turkish Cypriots into
the police force.

The Secretary-General's mid-June report on the first
three months of UNFICYP's operation stressed that the
continued arms build-up on the island cast doubt on
the Force's ultimate ability to prevent local violence.

[80] U.N. Doc. S/5671 Annex I, April 29, 1964, and see U.N. Doc.
S/5679, May 2, 1964.
   [81] U.N. Doc. S/5679.   [82] *Ibid.*   [83] *Ibid.*

Thant criticized both parties for actions he believed prejudicial to order on the island, including the taking of hostages and arms smuggling.[84] Decrying the report as "biased," Turkish officials insisted that its conclusions were based on "wrong and misleading information supplied by General Gyani."[85] On the basis of the Secretary-General's report, the Council unanimously extended UNFICYP's mandate for a second three-month term in a resolution[86] sponsored by the same five states who had drafted the two March resolutions. Both Cypriot parties expressed satisfaction with the Council's action. As UNFICYP began its second tour of duty in late June 1964, the tendency of all parties to buy time by adhering to fixed policy positions emerged more strongly. The conscription order that enlarged the Greek Cypriot police force to over 15,000 men and General Grivas' return to the island seemed to bear out Thant's assertion that the Cypriot government feared that the situation would become frozen in a manner contrary to its aim of regaining control over the whole island.

While the efforts of UNFICYP to restore order persisted, attempts to work toward a political solution to the island's disorders found the Greek and Turkish Cypriot communities seeking international support for their respective claims. Pressing for Assembly discussion of the internal conflict, the Archbishop reinforced his denunciation of the two treaties with unilateral pronouncements of dubious legal validity. Thus, in a letter to the *New York Times*, Zenon Rossides, Cyprus's U.N.

[84] U.N. Doc. S/5764, Corr. 1 and 2, June 15, 1964, paras. 21, 22, and 23.

[85] The *New York Times*, June 18, 1964.

[86] Security Council Resolution S/5778, June 20, 1964.

delegate argued that in voting for the admission of Cyprus to the United Nations the three guarantor powers
abdicated any claim to enforce the treaties; as a member of the United Nations, Cyprus enjoys "equal rights
of full independence and sovereignty . . . as prescribed
by the Charter—including, of course, the right of self-
determination."[87] Rossides argued that provisions of the
treaties that conflict with the Charter are rendered in-
valid under Article 103. Carrying these arguments to
their logical conclusion would entail abrogation of the
Austrian State Treaty as well as the Cyprus treaties.
The Charter makes no presumption about the automatic
invalidation of treaties concluded before a state joins
the Organization, although Article 103 does place the
Charter at the top of a hierarchy of international agreements. Moreover, the Charter does not "prescribe" the
"right of self-determination" in Article 4[88] or in any other
article. The Greek Cypriots continued to assert that the
Zurich-London agreements produced an unworkable
constitution granting excessive rights to the Turkish
Cypriot minority and that the arrangement was "foisted"
on an unwilling Greek Cypriot party. Completing their
arguments based on the Charter, the Greek Cypriots insisted that Turkey's right of intervention under the
Treaty of Guarantee conflicted with Article 2:4 and Article 2:7 and that "an act which is forbidden by the Char-

[87] The *New York Times*, June 26, 1964.
[88] Article 4 states:
"1. Membership in the United Nations is open to all other peace-
loving states which accept the obligations contained in the present
Charter and, in the judgment of the Organization, are able and willing to carry out these obligations.
"2. The admission of any such state to membership in the United
Nations will be effected by a decision of the General Assembly upon
the recommendation of the Security Council."

ter cannot be legalized by agreement of the parties thereof."[89]

After a temporary lull during which it appeared that both Makarios and the Greek government had abandoned the idea of *enosis*, Premier Papandreou revived the old conception in new dress, stressing "moderation" and "legality." In announcing with Makarios a ten-point program geared to direct attention away from Turkish Cypriot charges of Greek Cypriot brutality, the Greek statesman outlined a large and long-range role for the United Nations, including the possible occupation of Cyprus by UNFICYP for several years to ensure pacification; enactment of a U.N. guaranteed statute to protect the minority rights of the Turkish Cypriot community; and a U.N. supervised referendum to ascertain the majority's wishes for union with Greece.[90]

The positions of the Turkish Cypriot minority and the Turkish government continued to harden during the first three months of UNFICYP's operations and the first weeks of Sakari Severi Tuomioja's term as U.N. mediator. The Turkish Cypriots, at a disadvantage in the councils of regional or international organization where they have no official standing, relied upon vocal Turkish representation in NATO and the United Nations to overcome any difficulties in securing a hearing for their claims. The Turkish community's spokesmen asked for partition of the island with each community to be governed separately. In answer to Makarios' claims, the Turkish government and the Turkish Cypriots alleged that the Greek Cypriot leadership had failed to implement the Constitution and that the proposed amend-

[89] U.N. Doc. S/P.V. 1098, February 27, 1964, p. 68.
[90] The *New York Times*, May 11, 1964.

ments were prohibited by Article 182 of the Constitution. They argued that the two treaties were not subject to unilateral abrogation and that without them Cyprus could not have achieved independence from Britain. They charged the Greek Cypriot government with calculated policies of exclusion and oppression designed to drive the minority from the island. As the conflict progressed throughout the spring of 1964, Turkish Cypriot policy positions based on retention of the two treaties became increasingly untenable. The United States and Britain, as well as Greece and the Greek Cypriot community, ruled out a return to the status quo ante-bellum.

The personal mediation efforts of President Johnson in June 1964 failed to yield any positive results. No common ground among the various advocates of plebiscite, partition, *enosis*, double *enosis*, emigration, population exchange, a unitary state, and a federal structure with minority guarantees appeared to exist. Faced with domestic discontent over Cyprus, Greek and Turkish officials adhered to rigid positions in order to gain time before acceding to direct negotiations. Each party had stated its opposition to solutions put forward by other parties. Attempts to achieve partition on a municipal level had failed due to lack of a clear territorial separation of the two communities. Alternative proposals—emigration of the minority to Turkey or resettlement on Cyprus—raised questions of land redistribution, economic compensation, and population dislocation, questions that would arise in a federal arrangement in which Turkish Cypriot security might be difficult to guarantee. The absence of good will on both sides continued to make adoption of a federal state with minority rights and majority rule seem unlikely. Additional impediments to the task of conceiving and implementing a political solution to the island's communal discord included the question of the Communist Party's role in Cyprus and possible connections to NATO via Greece, Turkey, and Britain.

As behind-the-scenes negotiations aimed at seeking a political solution continued, tension on the island began to mount in July 1964. The presence of UNFICYP on the island had not resulted in an amelioration of conditions. The Greek Cypriots managed to prevent the Turkish communities from receiving supplies, and both sides were importing arms from abroad. After a series of Greek Cypriot attacks on Turkish Cypriot positions in northwest Cyprus, Turkish air force jets undertook air strikes against the forces of the Greek Cypriots. When the issue came before the Security Council, on a protest of the Makarios government, the Turkish delegate argued that the strikes were provoked by Greek Cypriot attacks, aided by large-scale military reinforcements. The Greek delegate asserted that unless the Turkish strikes ended, Greece would assist Cyprus by military means. The Turkish government was placed on the defensive in Council debate. Turkey's air strikes, after months of threatened military intervention, aroused hostile comments, especially from the new states and the Soviet Union. After charge and countercharge filled the Council chambers,[91] a British-American draft resolution calling for an immediate cease-fire and restoration of peace was adopted, by a vote of 9-0-2, with the Soviet Union and Czechoslovakia abstaining. The resolution,

[91] See Security Council, *Official Records*, Nineteenth Year, 1142nd-1143rd Meetings (August 8 and 9, 1964).

confirming earlier Council directives of March 4th and
13th and June 20th, called upon all states to "refrain
from any action that might exacerbate the situation or
contribute to the broadening of hostilities."[92] Both Cyprus and Turkey informed the President of the Council
of their acceptance of the cease-fire appeal, and the
Secretary-General decided to withhold a report of the
incidents of the fighting which had taken place on the
island since August 5th, despite the presence of the
U.N. Force there. Reports of additional hostilities led to
the expression of a consensus of views in the form of
a statement by the President of the Security Council
calling for adherence to the August 9th resolution and
a strengthening of UNFICYP in zones under military
attack.

As UNFICYP began its sixth month of duty, the Secretary-General issued a warning that the Force would
have to be withdrawn if additional financial support for
the peace-keeping operation failed to materialize.[93] The
seriousness of the situation was underscored by fears of
violence if the projected rotation of Turkish troops was
carried out over the opposition of the Cyprus government. Under the mandate given to UNFICYP, the Force
had no responsibility for Greek and Turkish contingents
on Cyprus, for these troops had never been incorporated
into the U.N. operation.

When the Council met in September to consider an
extension of UNFICYP for a third three-month period, a
report issued by the Secretary-General informed member-states that a withdrawal of the Force would lead to

[92] Security Council Resolution S/5868, August 9, 1964.

[93] UNFICYP completed its fifth month of operation with 6,211
men serving on Cyprus, police units totalling 174 and military personnel 6,037.

"utter disaster on the island."[94] At the same time, Thant warned that in the event of a further extension, "there will be serious need for at least some clarification as to actions that the Force may take in the discharge of its mandate."[95] In his conclusion, the Secretary-General summed up the events of the preceding three months' activity in terms worthy of detailed mention:

> UNFICYP was given a very heavy responsibility without any precise definition of its general mandate to guide it so that it might know clearly just what it is entitled to do and how far it may go, particularly in the use of force. This inadequacy and lack of clarity in the mandate of the Force has been, obviously, a handicap to its operation. The Force, of course, has been subjected to much pressure from those, on the one hand, who would wish it to go much further than it has gone, particularly in the employment of armed force, and those on the other, who feel that at times the Force tries to go too far on the territory of a sovereign state.[96]

Thant also stated his view that while the Force had not been able to prevent a recurrence of fighting, it had assisted in bringing open clashes under control before they could escalate into island-wide or larger hostilities. The Force, in the Secretary-General's opinion, had made a contribution to the restoration of law and order on Cyprus and to a partial return to normal conditions by such activities as opening up roads and aiding in the lifting of sieges directed against the Turkish Cypriot communities, although the frequent lack of cooperation

---

[94] U.N. Doc. S/5950 and Add. 1,2, September 10, 1964, para. 229.
[95] *Ibid.*, para. 232.
[96] *Ibid.*, para. 215.

of both Cypriot communities hampered U.N. efforts. The lack of cooperation stemmed from differing conceptions of what a return to normal conditions signified, Thant explained. The Force was attempting to steer a course midway between the lines suggested by opposing sides in the civil war; the Force could not, in the Secretary-General's view, accept the position of the Turkish Cypriots that armed force should be used by UNFICYP to restore the constitutional situation obtaining before the outbreak of violence, and that acts taken by the Cypriot government should be considered illegal. Nor could the Force accept the view of the Cyprus majority government that UNFICYP should be used as an arm of that group to quell the rebellion. Thant stated the dilemma posed by the field situation succinctly:

> The plain fact, therefore, is that the United Nations Force in Cyprus is in the most delicate position that any United Nations mission has ever experienced, for it is not only in the midst of a bitter civil war but it is dangerously interposed between the two sides of that war.[97]

Weighing the evidence presented by both sides, Thant argued that in view of the security situation resulting from the threats of Turkish intervention, tension was unavoidable. Yet he insisted that the imposition of economic restrictions on the Turkish Cypriot minority was not justified by these threats, and he recorded the United Nations' assistance to the stricken minority communities on the island. Thant was quick to condemn the Turkish government for its August aerial attacks and as quick to castigate the Cyprus govern-

[97] *Ibid.*, para. 221.

ment for its interference with UNFICYP's freedom of movement, noting that these restrictions attested to a lack of trust and good faith. In recommending an extension of UNFICYP, Thant declared that "a civil war is the worst possible situation in which a United Nations peace-keeping force can find itself"[98] and cautioned that the steady arms build-up, the intransigent positions of interested parties, and the precarious financial underpinning of the Force required the Council's immediate attention. After a series of eight meetings in which familiar claims and counterclaims were rehearsed in the light of the Secretary-General's report, the Council unanimously reaffirmed its prior resolutions on Cyprus.[99] But Soviet and Cypriot objections made a further clarification of the Force's mandate and financing impossible.

Several events in the next month eased the situation outlined in the Secretary-General's pessimistic report. Thant reached agreement with the Cypriot and Turkish governments for UNFICYP to take control of the Kyrenia road. An arrangement for the 650-man Turkish army contingent to be placed under U.N. control was announced. This arrangement was to be subject to the maintenance of security for the Turkish Cypriot minority and the agreement of the Turkish Cypriot leadership. Yet the consensus in the Council which had made an extension of UNFICYP to late December possible was reached only at the cost of concessions to the Soviet Union. If the Force were to continue its operations, Thant would have to run the Force under the vague March 4th mandate and the United States and Britain

---

[98] *Ibid.*, para. 229.
[99] Security Council Resolution S/5987, September 25, 1964.

would have to continue to donate funds for UNFICYP. Like Hammarskjöld, Thant had attempted to prod the Council into action by announcing that he would adopt a particular policy if the Council or Assembly did not specifically countermand his intentions. But in September, the Council, due to Soviet pressures, failed to approve the changes in the mandate and method of financing of UNFICYP desired by Thant. The arms agreement concluded between the Soviet and Cyprus governments detracted from the value of the arrangements for the rotation of Turkish troops.

On the first anniversary of the outbreak of intercommunal fighting in Cyprus, UNFICYP began another three-month tour of duty in an atmosphere of relative calm. The Council had unanimously voted to extend the Force again in December[100] on the same financial basis, because all Council members, including the Soviet Union, stated that they favored such an extension while discussions looking toward a long-term political solution continued. The expected announcement from Nicosia that Makarios would place the Cyprus question before the Assembly in its nineteenth session suggested that a new phase of U.N. involvement in the internal conflict was about to begin. The postponement of the session, delaying full-scale debate on the Cyprus question, exacerbated feelings between partisans of the hostile Cypriot communities.

The Greek Cypriot government, hoping for eventual Assembly endorsement of its views of Cypriot self-determination and territorial integrity, insisted that the December extension of UNFICYP should be the last. In the eyes of the majority government, UNFICYP con-

[100] Security Council Resolution S/6121, December 18, 1964.

tributed to a freezing of the status quo, permitting the Turkish Cypriots to run their own affairs. The Greek Cypriots, though strong enough to cope with the Turks militarily, held back from attack in hopes of avoiding the moral censure which would attend any additional fighting on the island while UNFICYP stood by. The Turkish Cypriots were still armed and on guard for any moves that might endanger their position. Surface calm could not conceal the underlying tensions that persisted on Cyprus. The "indispensable activities" of UNFICYP had succeeded in lessening the effect of some of the dislocation caused by protracted civil strife, Thant reported. But the Secretary-General explained that

> The basic factors of the Cyprus conflict remain essentially unchanged. Acute political conflict and distrust between the leaders of the two communities, and the passions stirred by the members of the two groups combine to create a state of potential civil war, despite the present suspension of actual fighting. This situation adversely affects the entire economy of the Island and causes some serious hardship for certain sections of the population, notably segments of the Turkish Cypriot community. The life and economy of the Island remain disrupted and abnormal, and it would be unrealistic to expect any radical improvement until a basic political solution can be found.[101]

Citing the "complex task" UNFICYP continued to perform as the "link and channel of communication between the two communities," Thant feared that if no political solution could be found, UNFICYP's task might become "static" and contribute to a dangerous

[101] U.N. Doc. S/6102, and Corr. 1 and 2, December 12, 1964, para. 237.

stalemate containing within it "the seeds of a relapse into chaos."[102]

Thant's description of the state of Cypriot political and economic life remained valid for the months preceding the submission of the U.N. mediator's report on March 30, 1965. The long-awaited report followed the rejection by the Makarios government of the Acheson Plan, which suggested that *enosis* with Greece and compensation to Turkey in the form of a military base or other territory form the basis for a solution. All substantive proposals had met stubborn resistance from parties who sensed that the moment for concessions had not arrived.

The report of Galo Plaza Lasso, who had become U.N. mediator after the death of Tuomioja, reviewed the history of the unsuccessful attempts to arrive at an agreed settlement to the Cyprus conflict pursuant to Security Council resolutions.[103] The report was notable for its firm opposition to the extreme positions taken by the majority and minority Cypriot communities. Ruling out *enosis*, partition, and federation as impractical, Plaza Lasso also drew attention to the apparent unworkability of the 1960 Constitution and the treaties of alliance and guarantee.[104] Although the separate talks held with the various parties concerned had failed to yield any indication of compromise, the mediator did not rule out the possibility of eventual settlement. He stressed the suitability of initial meetings[105] between the two Cypriot communities in order to find common ground. Noting the importance of iron-clad guarantees for the

[102] *Ibid.*, paras. 238-239.
[103] U.N. Doc. S/6253, March 26, 1965, paras. 15-112.
[104] *Ibid.*, paras. 130-165.   [105] *Ibid.*, para. 170.

safety of the Turkish Cypriot minority, Plaza Lasso suggested that a U.N. Commissioner, with staff, might be dispatched to the island to secure the confidence of both communities as they worked toward a merging of their separate identities into a single Cypriot state.[106]

A contribution to the maintenance of international security might result from these new arrangements, the mediator explained, if a different form of guarantee for a settlement could be established. The United Nations itself might act as the guarantor of the terms of settlement. The Organization might spell out in a resolution the terms of a settlement agreed to by the parties and then receive complaints of violation or problems in implementation.[107] In concluding his report, the mediator clarified the nature of his proposals:

> I have not felt it appropriate at this stage to set forth precise recommendation or even suggestions of a formal kind for a solution to the problem of Cyprus. I have tried instead by analyzing the positions of the parties and defining their objectives as I see them to make apparent certain directions which they themselves should explore in the search for a peaceful solution and an agreed settlement.[108]

The mediator urged that in the event of a satisfactory solution to the internal disorder, the terms of settlement should be presented to the Cypriot people for approval as a whole. In view of the difficult negotiations that would precede the announcement of such a solution, Plaza Lasso insisted that

> They should be asked to accept or reject it as a single package, and not in its various parts. This is because

[106] *Ibid.*, paras. 166-168.   [107] *Ibid.*   [108] *Ibid.*, para. 169.

any settlement which might be arrived at will necessarily be in the nature of a compromise involving
concessions to be made by both sides from their original positions. It seems to me inevitable that it will
have to be a carefully balanced series of agreements,
each relying on the other and all of them on the
whole.[109]

Moreover, he argued, if a majority vote against a final
settlement were to be registered, a new round of talks
would be needed to work out a different solution.

The circulation of the mediator's report provoked a
number of letters in which interested parties expressed
their interpretations of Plaza Lasso's observations and
suggestions. Archbishop Makarios, responding favorably
to the mediator's mention of "self-determination" for
Cyprus, supported the substance of the report and
stated his willingness to see the work of Plaza Lasso
continue.[110] The Turkish Cypriot leadership, in rejecting
the report's views as a basis for negotiations, reiterated
its demands for federation, stating that the proposed
guarantees set forth by the mediator would not be adequate to prevent possible domination of the island by
the Greek Cypriot majority.[111] The Greek government
expressed satisfaction with the substance of the proposals and urged a continuation of Plaza Lasso's efforts.[112]
Serious opposition from the Turkish government was
expressed in a letter decrying the report's inclusion of
views which, in that government's opinion, exceeded
the mediator's terms of reference as outlined in the
Council's resolution of March 4, 1964. Arguing that the

[109] *Ibid.*, para. 172.   [110] U.N. Doc. S/6275, Add.1, April 12, 1965.
[111] U.N. Doc. S/6279, April 3, 1965.
[112] U.N. Doc. S/6280, April 8, 1965.

mediator's suggestions did not represent "an agreed settlement," the Turkish government declared that it
would no longer support the efforts of Plaza Lasso to
find such a settlement. In reply to a letter from U Thant,
the Turkish government stated its willingness to support
continued U.N. attempts to seek an agreed settlement,
but emphasized its rejection of any further approaches
on the part of Plaza Lasso.[113] Thus Thant's assessment
of "stalemate" leading to possible "chaos" retained its
accuracy as a description of the Cyprus internal conflict in the absence of progress toward a political solution based on Plaza Lasso's views or on other suggestions.

The diplomatic lull following the reaction of principal
parties to the U.N. mediator's report was broken by
Archbishop Makarios' announced plan to revise the
electoral laws of Cyprus. The Turkish Cypriot minority
charged that the proposed alterations would deprive
that group of constitutional guarantees. When, at Turkey's request, the Security Council met to consider the
question, many delegates expressed the view that Makarios' action was illegal.[114] The representatives of Britain, France, and the United States drew attention to
Thant's recent report on conditions in Cyprus,[115] conditions of tension increased by the Greek Cypriot leader's

[113] U.N. Doc. S/6267 and Add. 1, March 31–April 6, 1965. When
Plaza Lasso subsequently resigned as U.N. mediator, he cited the
continued opposition of the Turkish government to his proposals as
a factor limiting his usefulness to the parties and to the Organization.
See U.N. Doc. S/7054, January 3, 1966.

[114] On June 26, 1965, the Council had extended UNFICYP's tour
for a six-month period pursuant to Thant's recommendation in his
June report on the Force's activities. See U.N. Doc. S/6426 and
Corr. 1, June 10, 1965.

[115] U.N. Doc. S/6569, July 29, 1965 and Add. 1 and 2, August 5
and 10, 1965.

policy decision. A week of debate was closed by passage of a draft resolution introduced by the six nonpermanent members of the Council. The compromise resolution,[116] in taking note of Thant's reports, reaffirmed the Council's first resolution on the Cyprus internal disorder, that of March 4, 1964. The Council appealed to all parties to avoid actions "likely to worsen the situation," but did not castigate the majority government for its proposal. Whether the Cyprus government would implement the revised laws remained unclear. Predictably, differing interpretations of the Council's resolution were issued by the representatives of Cyprus and Turkey. The Cypriot delegate argued that the Council's stress on "mediation" of communal differences signified that the resolution was not meant to cast blame on the Cyprus government, while the Turkish delegate contended that the resolution, in endorsing Thant's reports, condemned Makarios' action.

Controversial incidents in the Cypriot town of Famagusta preceded the deliberations of the Security Council in November 1965. In a familiar pattern, the Secretary-General's reports on the episode stimulated Turkish and Greek representatives to repeat charges that the other side had violated U.N. resolutions and had provoked a situation impeding a political settlement. The Council passed no resolution, but a statement by the President reiterated appeals for restraint and cooperation with the Organization. When in December the Council authorized another three-month continuation of UNFICYP, its resolution failed to provide new arrangements for financing.[117] In subsequent months,

[116] U.N. Doc. S/6603, August 10, 1965.
[117] U.N. Doc. S/7024, December 17, 1965.

the problem of adequate funds for the Force grew more acute, despite the fact that member-states continued to acknowledge the gravity of the conflict and to renew UNFICYP's mandate.[118]

The long-awaited discussion of the Cyprus question in the General Assembly did little to improve the prospects for an end to civil conflict. On the recommendation of the First Committee, the Assembly passed a resolution that was notable for its emphasis on the "independence" and "sovereignty" of Cyprus. The resolution, adopted by a vote of 47 to 5, with 54 abstentions,[119] indicated that many smaller states, especially newer African members, were in favor of a solution that would de-emphasize the roles of Greece and Turkey. Such an approach, while failing to command the support of all permanent members of the Security Council, accorded with Thant's conviction that the two Cypriot communities must play the leading role in seeking a political solution.[120] At the same time, the Secretary-General has sought to influence outside parties, particularly Greek and Turkish government officials. Through his representative in Cyprus, Dr. Carlos Bernardes, Thant proposed in May 1966 that the Greek and Turkish governments consider the possibility of a provisional settlement of the Cyprus conflict. Thant's ideas were not put forward as a formal plan. The Secretary-General suggested that Britain, France, the United States, and the U.S.S.R. guarantee an independent regime for Cyprus, and that the Zurich and London treaties be suspended for three

[118] On June 26th, the Security Council extended UNFICYP for a period of six months until December 26, 1966.

[119] General Assembly Resolution 2077 (XX), December 18, 1965.

[120] See for example U.N. Doc. S/7001, December 10, 1965, paras. 205-216.

to five years, after which negotiations on a permanent solution could begin. He proposed that the Security Council undertake to guarantee the rights of the Turkish minority and that the Council receive reports on the situation from a U.N. observer in Nicosia. The Greek government rejected the idea of a provisional solution on grounds that it would create additional problems. The Turkish government, in expressing a more favorable reaction to Thant's suggestions, subsequently agreed to meet with representatives of Greece for an exchange of views on all facets of Greek-Turkish relations.

The experience of the Organization in the Cyprus conflict has tended to reinforce the fact that "peace-keeping is a means and not an end. Peace-keeping, if successful, as it surely has been in Cyprus, can provide an atmosphere of quiet and buy a reasonable time for peace-making, for resolving the differences which give rise to the conflict. It is, however, and can only be, a first step towards pacific settlement." In Cyprus, as Thant has stressed, affairs "have not as yet advanced beyond this first stage. Indeed, it is becoming apparent that in order to move the situation effectively towards a solution, efforts at the highest level may have to be undertaken to resolve a problem which has lasted already far too long and which continues to pose a threat to the peace and stability of the eastern Mediterranean area."[121]

[121] U.N. Doc. S/7350, June 10, 1966, para. 172. Thant again reported a deadlock on the Cyprus question, an "uneasy truce," in December 1966. (See U.N. Doc. S/7611 and Add. 1, December 8, 1966.) In urging the Council to extend UNFICYP's mandate until June 1967, the Secretary-General expressed cautious optimism on the Greek-Turkish secret talks in progress. The Council's subsequent resolution reflected a similar view that such an extension might be the last one needed before a reduction or withdrawal of the Force.

The Dominican Republic

In neither the Congo nor Cyprus did the unilateral intervention of a superpower precede U.N. involvement. In the protracted civil strife in the Dominican Republic, the American military intervention shaped not only the course of the upheaval but also the response of the Organization. In neither the Congo nor Cyprus did the participation of regional organizations create jurisdictional problems for the United Nations once the general international organization had assumed major responsibility for coping with threats to the peace created by intrastate violence and for promoting political settlements. In the Dominican case, the United Nations' role was limited to discussion and observation. Lengthy and often inconclusive debates on the suitable functions for the OAS and the United Nations to perform in the conflict marked Council meetings.

The internal violence that erupted in the Latin American state in late April 1965 and its aftermath recalled earlier periods of domestic chaos and foreign interventions. Among its other interventions in Latin America in the early twentieth century, the United States in 1916 sent Marines to the Dominican Republic and established a military regime that governed until 1924. In 1930, General Rafael Trujillo Molina took power, and until his assassination in 1961 the dictator ruled in a manner notable for its cruelty. The unrest following Trujillo's murder appeared to be ended by the first free election in the country in thirty-eight years, held in February 1963. The new president, Juan Bosch, was regarded as a social reformer. He faced enormous problems of political reconstruction in a country whose parties and institutions lacked solidarity. Overthrown by a military coup seven months later, the Bosch administration was alleged to have suffered "Communist infiltration." This charge, an attempt to demonstrate a clear link between Bosch and Castroite elements in the Dominican Republic, was never fully substantiated.[122] Nor has the role played by the Pentagon and other American agencies in the September 1963 coup been made clear.[123] The Kennedy administration officially deplored the coup and temporarily severed diplomatic relations with the Dominican Republic.

A civilian junta backed by military support and led by Donald Reid Cabral assumed power after the coup. Its efforts to stabilize the country and gain wide support from the bulk of the population failed. On April 24, 1965, violence flared in the capital city of Santo Domingo as insurgent forces, who declared their intention of restoring Bosch to power under the Dominican Constitution, overthrew the Reid junta. A rival group of military leaders, led by General Elias Wessin y Wessin, who had been instrumental in the September 1963 coup, took to the streets to oppose the rebels. The events of the first days after the outbreak of hostilities were reported by journalists on the scene, who provided conflicting interpretations of the composition of the rebel group, the numerical strength of the opposing factions, and the attitude of American officials in the Dominican Republic toward the rival aspirants to power. While in the first two days after the coup it appeared that the

[122] For an account of events following Bosch's election see Theodore Draper, "The Roots of the Dominican Crisis," *The New Leader*, May 24, 1965, pp. 3-18.
[123] *Ibid.*, p. 11.

pro-Bosch forces were close to victory, the strafing of the capital by Dominican planes enhanced the position of the Wessin y Wessin forces. Nevertheless, the military junta lacked sufficient strength to quell the "constitutionalists." Thereafter different versions of the circumstances leading to the intervention of American forces were advanced by President Johnson, by Bosch in Puerto Rico, by rebel forces in Santo Domingo, and by Wessin y Wessin.

The dispatch of American airborne units and Marine reinforcements to the Dominican Republic on April 28th was explained by President Johnson on that day as a measure to "give protection to hundreds of Americans who are still in the Dominican Republic and to escort them safely back to this country."[124] The same reason was cited in a letter of April 29th sent to the President of the Security Council explaining the American action.[125] But on May 2nd, the President, in answering widespread criticism of the intervention, stated that

> the revolutionary movement took a tragic turn. Communist leaders, many of them trained in Cuba, seeing a chance to increase disorder, to gain a foothold, joined the revolution. They took increasing control. And what began as a popular democratic revolution, committed to democracy and social justice, very shortly moved and was taken over and really seized and placed into the hands of a band of Communist conspirators.[126]

[124] White House press release, April 28, 1965. Reprinted in *Department of State Bulletin*, LII, No. 1351 (May 17, 1965), 738.

[125] U.N. Doc. S/6310, April 29, 1965.

[126] White House press release, May 2, 1965. Reprinted in *Department of State Bulletin*, LII, No. 1351 (May 17, 1965), 744.

The President produced no evidence to support his assertion; but on May 5th the State Department released a list of fifty-five "Communist and Castroite" names to support the Johnson administration's claims of Communist take-over. The list, denounced by Bosch and rebel leaders, also was ridiculed by other governments and individuals critical of the American action.

The extent of hemispheric hostility to the unilateral American intervention emerged when the United States sought to involve the OAS in a peace-keeping role. An American draft resolution calling for a cease-fire was adopted by the Council of the OAS with no negative votes on April 30th.[127] Similarly, a second draft resolution introduced by the United States, in conjunction with Argentina, Brazil, Colombia, Guatemala, Mexico, and Peru, at the Tenth Meeting of the Consultation of the Ministers of Foreign Affairs, a resolution calling for the establishment of an OAS committee to investigate "all aspects of the situation in the Dominican Republic" and to assist in the arrangement of a cease-fire, was adopted on May 1st.[128] But prolonged negotiations were required to secure the adoption of an American draft resolution to establish an inter-American peace-keeping force. The creation of a regional military force, endorsed by the five-nation peace committee sent to Santo Domingo pursuant to the May 1st resolution, was opposed by Mexico, Uruguay, Chile, Ecuador, and Peru, by states with social and political systems more advanced than those in many other Latin American states. These

[127] Resolution of the Council of the Organization of American States, April 30, 1965. U.N. Doc. S/6315, May 1, 1965.

[128] Resolution of the Tenth Meeting of Consultation of Ministers of Foreign Affairs, Organization of American States, May 1, 1965. U.N. Doc. S/6319, May 3, 1965.

states, fearful that the American intervention might be a foretaste of other U.S. interventions in Latin American states experiencing domestic unrest, condemned the American action in the Dominican Republic and voted against the resolution. They decried the intervention as illegal under Article 17 of the OAS Charter[129] and scored the U.S. failure to consult the OAS before taking action. Their negative votes were not sufficient to defeat the plan; intensive behind-the-scenes discussions produced a bare two-thirds majority for the American proposal, as amended by five other Latin American states, who recorded the view that approval of OAS intervention in the Dominican Republic should not be construed as approval of the initial American intervention. Venezuela abstained on the resolution.

Approved by thirteen states plus a representative of the Dominican Republic (although the country had no legitimate government at the time), the resolution provided for an international force to be established, incorporating U.S. forces present in the Dominican Republic and units to be contributed by other members of the OAS. The resolution provided that the Force would operate under the authority of the Tenth Meeting of Consultation and would have as its purpose "that of co-operating in the restoration of normal conditions in the Dominican Republic, in maintaining the security of its inhabitants and the inviolability of human rights, and in the establishment of an atmosphere of peace and conciliation that will permit the functioning of demo-

---

[129] Article 17 of the OAS Charter states: "The territory of a state is inviolable; it may not be the object, even temporarily, of military occupation or of other measures of force taken by another state, directly or indirectly, under any grounds whatever."

cratic institutions."[130] The Security Council, under Article 54 of the Charter,[131] was informed of passage of the OAS resolution, as it had been informed of other actions taken by the regional body in the Dominican conflict.

The preference of the American government for OAS consideration of the Dominican disorder rather than U.N. involvement stemmed from its dominant position in the OAS and its disinclination to encourage the Soviet Union or Cuba to exploit the American military presence on the island for propaganda purposes. Thus when the Security Council debated the Dominican question in sixteen meetings from May 3rd to May 25th the American representative argued that the OAS should continue to exercise primary responsibility for attaining a permanent cease-fire and promoting a political solution to the disorder. In a series of statements to the Council, Stevenson defended the American intervention as necessary: "When hours and even minutes counted—there was no time for deliberate consultation and for the organization of international machinery which did not yet exist."[132] The American delegate repeated the claims of the U.S. government that its intervention was justified on humanitarian and legal grounds and stressed its interest in securing a settlement in accord with the wishes of the Dominican people.

[130] Resolution of the Tenth Meeting of Consultation of Ministers of Foreign Affairs of the Organization of American States, May 6, 1965, para. 2. U.N. Doc. S/6333, Rev. 1, May 7, 1965.

[131] Article 54 states: "The Security Council shall at all times be kept fully informed of activities undertaken or in contemplation under regional arrangements or by regional agencies for the maintenance of international peace and security."

[132] U.N. Doc. S/P.V. 1200, May 5, 1965, p. 12.

The Soviet and Cuban delegates led the vigorous attack on the American position. Condemning the U.S. action as "armed intervention in the internal affairs of the Dominican Republic," the U.S.S.R. on May 4th introduced a draft resolution calling on the United States to withdraw its troops from the Latin American country.[133] Later, after the resolution failed of adoption, the U.S.S.R. introduced amendments calling for American withdrawal into a draft resolution introduced by Uruguay on May 11th.[134] The Soviet representative insisted that under Article 39 the Council had the right to deal with the American "fait accompli" in the Dominican Republic, with the U.S. "repression" of the Dominican people, with its manipulation of the OAS, and with its "ludicrous" explanations of the violations of Articles 2:4 and 2:7 of the U.N. Charter and Article 17 of the OAS Charter.

The predictable Soviet and Cuban denunciations of American actions in Santo Domingo were by no means the sole expressions of distaste for the "Johnson doctrine" and for the American military action. While the Bolivian and British governments supported the OAS mediation efforts, the French government stressed that the American intervention by its scale, duration, and objectives ran the risk of exceeding the permissible limits of an operation to rescue American and other foreign nationals. Similarly, the representative of Jordan declared that the launching of the American intervention on the basis of a unilateral assessment of the situation might set a dangerous precedent. He stressed the desirability of U.N. control to restore normal conditions and order

[133] U.N. Doc. S/6328, May 4, 1965.
[134] U.N. Doc. S/6352, Rev. 1 and 2, May 12, 1965.

in the Dominican state. The delegate of Uruguay, in refusing to accept the reasons advanced to justify the American intervention, introduced a draft resolution expressing the Council's concern at developments in the Dominican Republic and calling upon contending factions in the country to progress toward a settlement of their differences.[135]

In objecting to the Uruguayan draft resolution, the United States again urged that the Council refrain from interposing itself into the conflict in view of the OAS participation. The United States, together with all other members of the Council, then approved a draft resolution introduced by the Ivory Coast, Jordan, and Morocco calling for a strict cease-fire and for the dispatch of a representative of the Secretary-General to the Dominican Republic "for the purpose of reporting to the Security Council on the present situation."[136] In successfully preventing passage of Council resolutions condemning its actions or giving the Secretary-General or the Security Council a larger role in the Dominican disorder, the United States retained its position as the central force in the internal conflict. Passage of the Council's resolution of May 14th followed the receipt of a cable signed by a rebel spokesman who identified himself as "Minister of Foreign Affairs of the Dominican Republic." The cable requested the Secretary-General to intervene to stop the advance of U.S. troops outside the Santo Domingo security zone established under OAS auspices.

While the Council debated new developments in the Dominican Republic, the United States secured the

[135] U.N. Doc. S/6346, May 11, 1965.
[136] U.N. Doc. S/6355, May 14, 1965.

resignation of Wessin y Wessin and his replacement by Brig. General Antonio Imbert Barreras, one of the two surviving assassins of Trujillo. Despite the continuing mediation efforts of the Papal Nuncio, the Secretary-General of the OAS, and the five-man OAS peace mission, whose powers had been broadened by directives of the OAS ministerial council, the Imbert military junta and the rebel forces under their provisional president, Colonel Caamaño Deño continued to fight in violation of an OAS-arranged cease-fire.

On May 18th, Dr. José Mayobre, Thant's personal representative, recommended to the Secretary-General that the Security Council act to bring about a cease-fire in view of Imbert's refusal to adhere to a truce.[137] Thant, in reporting to the Council on Mayobre's efforts to achieve a cease-fire, noted that Mayobre had drawn to the attention of U.S. officials the difficulties created by the American failure to prevent the movement of Imbert's forces and the consequences of the splitting of the rebel forces created by the security corridor.[138] Progress toward attainment of a cease-fire was reported by Thant in the next six days.[139]

On May 19th, the President of the Security Council informed member-states that a majority and a minority report had been received from the OAS five-man peace committee. The majority report, from which Panama dissented, criticized both the U.S. unilateral action in sending an American presidential mission under Mc-George Bundy to the Dominican Republic to seek a

[137] U.N. Doc. S/6365, May 18, 1965.

[138] U.N. Doc. S/6369, May 19, 1965.

[139] See U.N. Docs. S/6378, May 20, 1965; S/6371 and Add. 1 and 2, May 21-23, 1965; S/6380, May 24, 1965, and S/6386, May 26, 1965.

political solution, and the intervention of the United Nations, which, the report claimed, had "obstructed" the efforts of the OAS committee to carry out its mandate.[140] The committee recommended its own termination and its replacement by a representative of the OAS to mediate between the contending factions. The report also called upon the Security Council to suspend its activities in the Dominican Republic until regional efforts had been exhausted.

While U.S. officials continued to work with OAS authorities and with individual parties in an effort to restore a cease-fire and secure acceptance of a coalition regime excluding both Caamaño and Imbert from participation, the OAS and the Security Council resumed debate on the continuing crisis. American support for a coalition regime marked a shift from support of the Imbert junta the United States had placed in power and an apparent, though belated, acknowledgment of the depth of non-Communist endorsement of the rebel cause. The bitter fighting, intensified by the assault of junta forces against the rebel positions in Santo Domingo, increased American uneasiness over the slow progress recorded in building up the Inter-American Force. In an effort to spur other commitments, the United States formally turned over its forces, totalling 21,500 men, to the OAS command.[141]

The OAS repeated its urging of a permanent cease-fire in its resolutions of May 19th and 22nd.[142] In ac-

[140] U.N. Doc. S/6370 and Add. 1 and 2, May 19, 1965.

[141] See Notes No. 115 and 116 from Ambassador Ellsworth Bunker to the Assistant Secretary-General of the Organization of American States, May 15 and 22, 1965. Reprinted in *Department of State Bulletin*, LII, No. 1354 (June 7, 1965), 911-912.

[142] See U.N. Doc. S/6374, May 22, 1965.

cepting the majority recommendations of its five-man peace committee the OAS terminated the committee's mandate and entrusted its Secretary-General with the responsibilities of arranging a cease-fire, providing good offices to the parties, coordinating "insofar as relevant" his activities with those of Thant's representative, and reporting to the Tenth Meeting of Consultation the results of his negotiations.

The Security Council, continuing its deliberations, adopted a French draft resolution[143] requesting that the truce established on May 21st, temporarily ending fierce hostilities in Santo Domingo, be transformed into a permanent cease-fire. The French proposal eliminated references to the OAS; for this reason, the U.S. representative explained, he could not vote for it and would abstain. Contending that the Security Council's competence to deal with threats to international peace and security was not at issue, the U.S. delegate stressed that the OAS action in the Dominican Republic was not enforcement action and that therefore Security Council approval was not needed for it. Noting that the OAS was keeping the Council informed of its actions via the Secretary-General's representative and other means, Stevenson declared that "the purposes of the United Nations Charter will hardly be served if two international organizations are seeking to do things in the same place with the same people at the same time."[144] The United States, having submitted a draft resolution on May 21st calling for a strict cessation of fighting, encouragement of OAS efforts, and coordination of Mayobre's activities with those of José Mora, the OAS Secre-

---

[143] U.N. Doc. S/6376, May 22, 1965.
[144] U.N. Doc. S/P.V. 1217, May 22, 1965, p. 21.

tary-General,[145] withdrew its proposal on May 24th as
no longer pertinent in view of the new mandate given
to Dr. Mora by the Tenth Meeting of Consultation on
May 20th. The Security Council thus concluded the
first phase of its consideration of the Dominican disorder without extending the United Nations' role.

The U.S. government, in defending its actions during
the first month of its intervention, consistently denied
charges that American military or political authorities
were assisting the Imbert regime in the internal conflict. Said Stevenson before the Security Council on
May 19th,

> The allegation has been made again—I suspect for
> the seventh or eighth time—that the United States is
> giving aid to the Imbert forces and the Government
> of National Reconstruction, as it is called. I repeat
> that the United States has avoided scrupulously giv-
> ing military assistance either to the forces of the
> Government of National Reconstruction or the Con-
> stitutional Government of Colonel Caamaño. Not
> only has the United States refrained from giving aid
> to either side in this conflict, but we have prohibited
> the armed forces of either Imbert or Caamaño from
> using the zone of safety established under the OAS
> resolution as a refuge or sanctuary, or crossing the
> line of communication which connects the zone with
> the Duarte Bridge.[146]

The official versions of American conduct in the Dominican Republic were often at variance with the reports of U.S. commentators on the scene and in Wash-

[145] U.N. Doc. S/6373, May 21, 1965.
[146] U.N. Doc. S/P.V. 1212, May 19, 1965, p. 66.

ington. The shifts in the attitudes of U.S. policy-makers and in the behavior of American troops toward the factional groups in the hardening internal disorder were described by James Reston in late May in the following terms: "The Marines were to be neutral in the Dominican Republic, but were at first neutral on the side of the junta, and then on the side of the rebels, and then back again to the junta until a new order of 'strict neutrality' went out."[147] The reports from Santo Domingo conflicted with each other as some observers insisted that American forces, who held decisive power in the capital city, had failed to block the junta's assault on rebel positions and in fact abetted the move, while other correspondents appeared to accept the official denials from the Johnson administration.

When the Council resumed debate on the Dominican disorder on June 2nd, the Soviet Union, France, Uruguay, and Jordan recommended that the U.N. observer's role be enlarged in order to permit Mayobre to investigate alleged violations of human rights and violations of the cease-fire. The American delegate argued that such powers had not been requested by Mayobre and that the OAS Human Rights Commission should continue to investigate human rights cases. In urging the Council to support the OAS activities, Stevenson argued that duplication of effort would confuse the situation and perhaps encourage rival Dominican factions to play off U.N. and OAS investigating groups against each other. Britain, Malaysia, and Bolivia concurred with the American position. The debate was marked by repeated Soviet denunciations of the American intervention, especially after the circulation of reports that the Inter-

[147] The *New York Times*, May 23, 1965.

American Force had taken over additional territory in the rebel zone on June 15th and 16th.

The Council's June debate on the Dominican internal disorder proved inconclusive. Obvious disagreement precluded passage of draft resolutions endorsing OAS actions or calling for an enlarged U.N. role. In the Latin American country, economic dislocation as well as political discord prevented a rapid easing of tension between hostile factions. The OAS continued to operate on the scene, acting through a three-man mediation committee composed of the American, El Salvadorian and Brazilian ambassadors to the OAS. The relationship of the committee's mandate to provide good offices to all parties for purposes of reconciliation and recovery to Mora's prior mandate was left undefined. The committee held a series of talks with rebel leaders and junta officials, with individuals in the interior as well as in Santo Domingo, in an attempt to reach a settlement accommodating some of the demands of both principal parties to the internal disorder.

The rebel forces, confined to a small zone in Santo Domingo, continued to press for an expansion of the U.N. role rather than OAS mediation. Rebel leaders called for the restoration of the 1963 Constitution; reinstallation of the Chamber of Deputies and Senate elected December 20, 1962, and terminated by a military coup in September, 1963; formation of a government of "democratic personalities"; incorporation of officers loyal to Colonel Caamaño in the Dominican armed forces; and withdrawal of the United States and Latin American troops. Junta leaders, in control of more territory and in closer contact with the Inter-American Force and U.S. officials, wished to use OAS mediation efforts as a means of terminating rebel activity that prevented junta control of the entire country. The OAS proposed to both factions that they accept a peace plan providing for general elections under OAS supervision, to be held in six or nine months with all democratic political parties and leaders participating; formation of a provisional government that would serve until the elections; the return of all members of the regular armed forces to their barracks, where they would be subject to the authority of a civilian government and removed from political activity; the surrender to the OAS of all arms held by civilians, and a general amnesty for all participants in the strife, provided they laid down their arms; the continuation of the Inter-American peace force and of the Inter-American Commission on Human Rights; and diplomatic recognition by the American republics of the provisional government.[148]

The protracted efforts of the OAS mediation committee to form a transitional regime to govern until elections could be held were hampered by the distrust of rebel and junta leaders toward each other, by the pressure of extremist elements on both sides for a military solution, by the reluctance of business or professional men to accept positions in the provisional government, and by the tendency of each side to renege on promises made to OAS officials. Additional impediments to a solution of the internal disorder included disagreements over the form of the Institutional Act to serve as the provisional constitution, continuing infractions of the tenuous cease-fire, and alleged junta executions and torture of political opponents. In mid-July, when progress toward agreement on a political settlement of the civil strife had

[148] U.N. Doc. S/6457, June 18, 1965.

slowed, the Soviet Union again called for a Council meeting, contending that the Inter-American Force was planning moves against rebel forces.

The July Council debates resembled earlier meetings on the Dominican conflict in that the United States, the U.S.S.R., and Cuba repeated familiar charges and countercharges. Nor could the Council agree on a draft resolution to expand the U.N. role. The economic paralysis of the Dominican Republic and the tense military situation made the need for an early settlement essential. Nevertheless, the statements of representatives of both local parties to the Council indicated little flexibility. Both sides demanded a withdrawal of the Inter-American Force, charging that its presence constituted an illegal interference in the country's domestic affairs. The junta claimed it could restore order without OAS troops, while the rebels looked to the United Nations to redress a situation they regarded as favoring the junta.

The prevailing disagreement evident in Council debates was mirrored in the OAS. In early July, the U.S. government dropped its plan to press for the establishment of a permanent inter-American peace force at the Rio conference when it became clear that few Latin American countries favored the idea. In mid-July, the conference itself, scheduled to open on August 4th, was postponed indefinitely. The sharp division of opinion between the United States and the non-military governments of Latin America over the American intervention in the Dominican Republic, evident in the scant majority that voted for establishment of the OAS peace force, was apparent in the lack of response to the Force. Aside from Brazil, only the military dictatorships of Honduras,

Nicaragua, and Paraguay contributed troops; Costa Rica contributed police.

The tenuous restoration of public order on the island in September 1965, after the resignation of the Imbert junta and the installation of a provisional government under Dr. Hector Garcia Godoy, brought to a close the acute phase of civil strife in the small state. But friction between military and civilian authorities, coupled with social and economic dislocations, combined to create an atmosphere of instability in the months prior to the June 1966 elections for a new president. The Council's role throughout this period was confined to receiving U Thant's reports on political developments. With the election of Joaquin Balaguer as President, and the phased withdrawal of the Inter-American Force (completed in September 1966), international interest in Dominican affairs subsided.

Conclusion

In order to cope with widely acknowledged threats to international peace and security created by a breakdown of law and order in the Congo and in Cyprus, the Security Council authorized peace-keeping operations to assist in containing local violence and preventing external interventions. In both cases, the Organization sought to restore stability so that political solutions to internal violence could be fostered. In both cases, the inadequate size of the peace forces, the restrictions imposed on their use of arms, and complex logistical problems hindered U.N. efforts to contain local violence. While the restraint of outside parties contributed to the success of attempts to prevent large-scale unilateral interventions in behalf of rebels or incumbents, outsiders were able to affect the outcome of these disorders by sending arms or other aid clandestinely, by diplomatic backing in the United Nations and in bilateral or regional contexts, and by withholding support from the United Nations' collective undertaking. In both cases, incumbent governments sought to use U.N. forces in ways favorable to their own interests, despite the avowed non-interventionary stance of the field mission. In both cases, the Secretary-General and field personnel have experienced problems in translating vague mandates from the United Nations' political organs into terms applicable to fast-changing field circumstances.

In the Congo case, as events shifted the balance of forces in the internal conflict from one side to the other, third parties shifted their votes in the Assembly and Council, thereby creating uncertainties about the functioning of the field operation. ONUC became a stake in factional conflicts within the Congo, and the Secretary-General became a target for dissatisfied states whose national interests in the internal disorder were thwarted by the United Nations. Without the power to act as the sole authority in the strife-torn territory that lacked a viable, constitutional central government capable of imposing order, the Organization was compelled to act in the service of an ill-defined, controversial policy in cooperation with the superpower that was providing the Force with equipment and support. A choice was made between rival factional groups so that ONUC could perform its tasks, tasks that involved positive as well as negative facets. ONUC became embroiled in cold-war politics after its use of force pursuant to Council resolutions based on a shifting political consensus. A breakdown in civil-military and headquarters-field relations further marred the operation, already seriously hampered by strained relations between U.N. field personnel and representatives of the host state.

The Organization's first peace-keeping operation in an internal disorder involving a breakdown of law and order created as many problems as it purported to resolve. Political objections, such as those voiced by the Soviet Union and later France, resulted in a grave financial crisis that threatened to wreck the entire institution. Buffers like the Advisory Committee could not shield the office of the Secretary-General from pressures affecting its direction of the field mission. The resumption of externally abetted rebellion prior to ONUC's departure underscored the "holding operation" character of the United Nations' four-year effort and dramatized U Thant's warning that "the United Nations cannot permanently protect the Congo or any other country from the internal tensions and disturbances created by its own organic growth toward unity and nationhood."[149]

The U.N. peace-keeping endeavor in Cyprus has profited from the mistakes made in the Congo. The Force's functions have been limited to those involved in controlling violence and discouraging national interventions, with responsibilities for long-term political solutions left to U.N. mediators. Cyprus, in some ways a less vital stake than the Congo for big-power competition, a state in disorder yet possessing a central government in command, has posed peculiar problems of its own for the Organization. But the Secretary-General has found it easier to obtain legitimate political guidance from the Security Council; and interested third parties, Greece and Turkey, have yielded to restraints

[149] U.N. Doc. S/5784, June 29, 1964, p. 42.

urged by more powerful states with whom they are allied. Adequate financing and advance planning remain unsolved problems for future peace-keeping enterprises. The stop-gap, ad hoc measures employed in the Congo and Cyprus cases are unsatisfactory if the Organization is to play a more significant peace-keeping role in containing local violence and preventing external interventions in internal disorders judged to threaten international peace and security.

The problems encountered in the U.N. efforts to control violence in intrastate conflicts may be contrasted with those experienced in the United Nations' continuing efforts to prevent additional hostilities between Egypt and Israel. From 1956 to 1967, UNEF assisted in enforcing a pause between two contiguous states who might have drifted into a resumption of violence susceptible to rapid extension. The fact that the two parties to the dispute, Israel and Egypt, possess stable governmental administrations facilitated the Organization's task of observing an agreed cease-fire. The exclusion of the permanent members of the Security Council from participation in UNEF's field operations placed responsibilities for continued maintenance of the Force on the smaller states, and the duties UNEF performed did not require military support beyond that which smaller states were able to provide.

In some intrastate disorders, as in the Congo case, the United Nations may face a breakdown in governmental authority, a power vacuum or situation of domestic anarchy with possible intrusion of outside parties supporting incumbents or insurgents. In other intrastate conflicts, as in the Cyprus case, a centralized governmental authority may remain intact. Yet, as a party to

the conflict, the challenged government may complicate the task of containing violence by taking actions
designed to upset a military or political status quo. In
internal disorders involving a partial or complete breakdown of law and order, an international organization
like the United Nations or a regional body like the OAS
may be hampered by the need to select a candidate for
the order-giving function. Such a selection invites debate and potential conflict within the United Nations'
political councils if one or both the superpowers or other
states refuse to refrain from pressing narrow national
interests. Similar difficulties may beset a regional organization, as the OAS participation in the Dominican
breakdown of law and order attests.

The U.N. conciliation efforts in the Congo and Cyprus
cases suggest that the Organization's capacity to devise
and implement political solutions to internal disorders
is limited. The Organization, through recommendations
of the Assembly and Council or subsidiary bodies, may
propose solutions, but states dispose. The Congo disorder demonstrates that the task of finding an acceptable settlement increases in complexity as more parties
develop interests in the continuing conflict. Similarly,
the Cyprus conflict, with many parties involved through
historic interests, has defied solution via bilateral, regional, or multilateral techniques.

No two internal conflicts present the self-determination question or human rights problems in exactly the
same way. If the United Nations does assume an active
role in seeking political solutions, a degree of improvisation is inevitable. In the post-independence internal
conflicts of the Congo and Cyprus, the Organization's
councils have promoted solutions in conformity with

political considerations, although economic and legal factors also figured to some extent in the Thant Plan and in Plaza Lasso's proposals for Cyprus. In colonial wars, the invocation of self-determination as a "right" has fallen on sympathetic ears in the Assembly. In the post-colonial internal conflicts, the receptivity of member-states to the notion of self-determination has varied with the particular circumstances of the case at hand. The majority rejected such a claim on the part of Katanga, partly because the secessionist province was associated with Belgian interests. The Western states who revealed a deeper concern with the future of the Congo as an in-dependent state rejected the self-determination claim because it threatened to reduce the possibility of politi-cal and economic survival for the Congo to an unac-ceptable level. The Cypriot government's reliance on the right of self-determination has been received with less opposition, despite its doubtful legality. The conse-quences of an eventual settlement in tacit accord with some idea of self-determination do not appear as threatening as they did in the Congo case. Although the U.N. mediator's proposals eliminate ethnic parti-tion or double *enosis* as final solutions, the fact that these proposals have been rejected by the Turkish gov-ernment suggests that either partition or double *enosis* may receive renewed consideration at some future date.

The United Nations' success in assisting parties to find political solutions to the Congo and Cyprus con-flicts has been reduced by the ability of incumbent gov-ernments to resist pressures from older states while gathering support for their policies from the newer states who fear internal unrest in their own territories. The international society's experiences in the Congo,

Cyprus, and Dominican cases reveal the extent to which the attitudes of interested local parties and foreign sponsors create uncertainties that jeopardize solutions framed in multilateral, regional, or bilateral settings. Settlements imposed by outside parties prior to the granting of independence, or afterward when internal conflict has erupted, carry with them the seeds of future discord. The type of solution advanced in the political organs of international organizations and regional bodies will reflect the views of member-states with different interests in the outcome of the conflict. Such solutions may be unsuited to the politics of the country experiencing internal strife, especially if that country is a modernizing Asian, African, or Latin American state.

In the Congo and Cyprus, the United Nations undertook responsibilities for finding and implementing political solutions. Comparable functions were assumed by the OAS in the Dominican Republic. The results of U.N. efforts in the Congo and Cyprus led to serious controversy within the Organization. The OAS encountered comparable internal friction as a result of its involvement in the Dominican Republic. In assuming responsibilities more extensive than those involved in assisting the parties to negotiate, international organizations run the risk of hindering their effectiveness in performing other political tasks. The least controversial and potentially most effective role the United Nations and regional organizations can play in promoting solutions to internal conflicts involving a breakdown of law and order is a limited one: creating circumstances favorable to negotiations between parties. By offering guidance and assistance regardless of the legal status of

171

the parties, by refusing to assume the burden of formulating or imposing political solutions, the United Nations and regional organizations may perform acts of mediation or conciliation. By virtue of its purposes and principles, the United Nations has a vested interest in the restoration of stable conditions, but it need not have a vested interest in a particular solution to an internal disorder. So long as potential or actual threats to international peace and security are contained, even incompletely or temporarily, neither the United Nations nor regional organizations need damage their prestige by becoming committed to unworkable formulas.

CHAPTER IV

The United Nations Role in Proxy Wars and Internal Conflicts Involving Charges of External Aggression or Subversion

THE competitive interests that have limited the Organization's effectiveness in colonial wars and in internal conflicts involving a breakdown of law and order have circumscribed its role in intrastate disorders whose distinguishing feature is a proxy character or alleged external aggression or subversion. The actions of third-party states—the superpowers in Greece, Guatemala, Hungary, Lebanon, Laos, and Vietnam, and Egypt, and Saudi Arabia in Yemen—have increased the danger to international stability when violence has erupted in these countries. In these disorders, as in others touching on vital interests, the Charter's provisions and the Organization itself as it has developed as a political institution have represented at best a partial embodiment of national objectives for third-party states. Nevertheless, in promoting desired results to these conflicts, the superpowers and other states have found uses for the Organization, albeit non-extensive ones. The United Nations have served as a forum for debate and propaganda and on occasion as a mechanism for investigation and observation, thereby enabling the majority of member-states to express an international concern if not a commitment to a particular outcome. The uses to which states have put the Organization have varied with the nature and extent of the third-party participation; but a pattern of response has developed that excludes large-scale peace-keeping operations and U.N. responsibilities for securing particular political solutions.

Greece

The unrest in Greece after the end of World War II found the United States faced with difficult policy choices. The British withdrawal from parts of the Middle East, coupled with the devastation of the war and Stalin's take-over in Eastern Europe, left Greece, and other countries in the region bordering on lands controlled or threatened by the Soviet Union, prone to external subversion as well as to civil disturbances. The United States was interested in using the United Nations as an instrument for exposing what the American government regarded as serious threats to the peace, threats created by the activities of Albania, Bulgaria, and Yugoslavia along the Greek frontiers.

On December 3, 1946, Greece requested the Security Council to consider the situation in northern Greece arising from aid allegedly supplied to Greek guerrillas by the three northern neighbors. The Council had previously discussed a complaint of the U.S.S.R., in January 1946, charging that the continued presence of British troops constituted an interference in Greek affairs likely to endanger international peace and security. The Council discussed the complaint, took note of the charge and the replies from Britain and Greece refuting Soviet assertions, but passed no resolution. In August 1946 the Ukrainian S.S.R. complained that the policies of the Greek government constituted a threat to peace. Greece, denying these charges, claimed that Albania had provoked a series of frontier incidents. Again, no Council resolution was adopted. In September, the Albanian government asked the Council to take up the matter of alleged violations of the Greek-Albanian border by Greek soldiers. The Council was unable to agree on any of the four draft resolutions proposed. By December 1946 the interests of the United States and the U.S.S.R. in the Greek disturbances had become clarified. Each superpower had shown a concern for the propaganda advantages that could be gained by securing U.N. condemnation of the other's activities, or the actions of local parties favorable to the other's interests.

On December 19, 1946, the Security Council established a commission of investigation empowered to visit Greece, Albania, Yugoslavia, and Bulgaria in order to "ascertain facts relating to alleged border violations" and to "elucidate causes and nature of border violations."[1] These directives were more extensive than the functions outlined in Article 34. The United States took a broad view of the Commission's functions and, with other permanent members of the Council, participated in its work. The Commission established its own procedures in the field, conducting meetings over a period of months in Greece, Bulgaria, and Yugoslavia. The Commission's report to the Council contained two sets of recommendations because Poland, the Soviet Union, and France objected to the majority's conclusion that Yugoslavia, and to a lesser extent Bulgaria, had supported guerrilla warfare in Greece by such means as training refugees and providing political instruction.[2] The Commission concluded that while the general unrest in Greece could not be characterized as civil war,

[1] Security Council, *Official Records*, First Year, Second Series, No. 28, 87th Meeting (December 19, 1946), p. 700.

[2] See Security Council, *Official Records*, Second Year, Special Suppl. No. 2, Vol. I, pp. 147-152.

Greece's three northern neighbors were responsible for subversive activity.[3] Russia's rejection of the majority's findings rested on political grounds, but the French disagreement stemmed from the view that the Council and not the Commission should reach conclusions on the evidence collected.[4] Some of the Commission's conclusions looked to future events. The majority proposed that the Council should regard any future incursions of armed bands from one country to another as a threat to international peace and security.[5] Other suggestions were specific and included provisions for the formation of a new body to assist in promoting peaceful relations among the parties, and to consist of representatives from countries other than the four interested parties and permanent members of the Council.[6] The new body would assist in the formation of new conventions and agreements for borders and voluntary transfer of minorities.[7]

Following the completion of the Commission's task, the United States proposed that the Council establish a subsidiary organ to implement the Commission's recommendations. This subsidiary body would function as an organ of investigation and conciliation and would be authorized to enter the territory of any of the involved parties and to summon witnesses. In making its proposal, the United States rejected a Syrian viewpoint that would have limited the activities of the Commission of Investigation to the preliminary finding that a dispute or situation existed and was likely to endanger international peace and security. The American representative declared,

[3] *Ibid.*, pp. 106ff.   [4] *Ibid.*, pp. 148, 156.   [5] *Ibid.*, p. 154.
[6] *Ibid.*, p. 155.   [7] *Ibid.*, pp. 155-156.

It seems to my delegation that it is inherent in the powers conferred by Article 34 and conferred by other provisions of the Charter relating to the duties and functions of the Security Council that it may continue to make such investigations as long as it thinks the situation exists.[8]

While most states disagreed with the American contention that the new body could be established under Article 24, there was scant support for the Soviet position that its powers would exceed the provisions of Article 34 and that the first Commission's report had exhausted the possibilities of Council investigation. The French delegate emphasized that the Council's powers were not circumscribed by initial findings:

I feel that if the Security Council has had the power to initiate an investigation for the purpose of obtaining information and of ascertaining whether a situation endangering peace exists, it is reasonable to suppose that it can continue this investigation when the situation itself seems likely to continue. . . . it would be paradoxical I think that an investigation could be continued if it did not find there was a threat to the peace, if it left the matter in doubt, but could not be continued in the most serious situation, that is, one in which a threat to the peace was found to exist.[9]

[8] Security Council, *Official Records*, Second Year, No. 61, 162nd Meeting (July 22, 1947), p. 1424.

[9] *Ibid.*, p. 1426. Although at the San Francisco Conference, the sponsoring governments and France had agreed to consider ordering of an investigation as a non-procedural matter requiring the concurrence of all the permanent members of the Council, debates on the Greek question were evidence that some members wished to regard the decision to establish a sub-committee to gather evidence and

On March 12, 1947, President Truman had announced that the United States would undertake a unilateral commitment to assist the Greek and Turkish governments in resisting Communist subversion. The Soviet Union, criticizing the American move, proposed that aid be given through the United Nations by means of a special commission, but the proposal was rejected by the Council on April 18th. The divergent positions of the Western states and the Soviet Union made agreement on additional Council resolutions impossible. The Council's vote to remove the Greek question from the list of matters of which it was seized ended the first phase of the United Nations' concern with subversion directed against Greece.

The Assembly, led by the United States, took up the Greek question at its second session. In a resolution calling on the Albanian, Bulgarian, and Yugoslav governments to refrain from aiding Greek guerrillas, the Assembly asked that the three states cooperate with Greece in resolving differences over frontiers, refugees, and minority groups and suggested normal diplomatic relations be established.[10] The Assembly also authorized the formation of the United Nations Special Committee on the Balkans (UNSCOB). This group operated without the participation of two of its eleven members—Poland and Russia—from 1947 to 1951. Its reports to the Assembly covered its unsuccessful efforts to obtain the cooperation of all four Balkan governments and stressed the continuing threat to Greek independence

report as a procedural matter under Article 29. The Soviet Union then and later consistently argued against that interpretation, asserting that the decision to undertake an investigation by commission or subcommittee is a substantive matter.

[10] General Assembly Resolution 109, October 21, 1947.

and territorial integrity. Neither Yugoslavia, Bulgaria, nor Albania called on UNSCOB for assistance in setting up negotiations with Greece for settlement of border or refugee problems.

Marshal Tito's defection from the Soviet camp in 1948 led to an easing of subversive activity against Greece directed from Yugoslavia; but UNSCOB reported in 1949 that aid from Albania and Bulgaria continued to endanger peace in the region. UNSCOB's last report in 1951 stated that the aid to guerrillas had expanded and was being furnished by Czechoslovakia, Hungary, Poland, and Rumania, as well as Bulgaria and Albania. When the Assembly terminated the Special Committee's mandate in 1951, it created still another body—the Balkan Sub-Commission under the aegis of the Peace Observation Commission.[11] This Sub-Commission's authority was more limited than that of UNSCOB, for it could dispatch observers only on request of states consenting to their entrance. But it could also visit areas being observed and report findings to the Peace Observation Commission and the Secretary-General.

The significant development in the Greek unrest was the bolstering of the incumbents' cause that resulted from implementation of the Truman Doctrine and Yugoslavia's shift in policy. The investigations conducted under U.N. auspices suffered from the non-cooperation of some major parties to the dispute, but the flow of reports to the Council and Assembly served to expose the subversive character of the Greek disorder, substantiating charges advanced in the political councils by the majority of Western states. The propa-

[11] General Assembly Resolution 508 (VI), December 7, 1951.

ganda value of the reports should not be underestimated, especially since in the early days of cold-war rivalry within the Organization, as in the days of increased membership, propaganda advantages were eagerly sought by the competing superpowers.

Guatemala

Internal violence involving charges of external aggression again confronted the Council in June 1954 when the Minister for External Relations of Guatemala asked that the Council take measures to stop hostile overflights of Guatemalan territory and the entry of foreign forces into that Latin American state. The Guatemalan government's charge that the United States had supported an invasion against it launched from Honduras and Nicaragua was widely accepted in the press.[12] The incumbent Arbenz regime was regarded as pro-Communist by the United States; the Guatemalan government favored the Council's jurisdiction, fearing that American officials would use the OAS to secure its overthrow if the matter were to be handled by the regional organization.[13]

The Soviet Union, also pressing for Council priority under Articles 34 and 35 so that it could exert some influence on the outcome, objected to an American-backed draft resolution to refer the question to the OAS. The French government proposed that a final paragraph be added to the draft resolution calling for the cessation of violence, without prejudice to any measures the OAS might take. The amended draft resolu-

[12] Inis Claude, "The OAS, the UN and the United States," *International Conciliation*, No. 547 (March 1964), p. 31.
[13] *Ibid.*, p. 28.

tion was vetoed by the Soviet Union, but when the French proposal was reintroduced as a separate draft resolution it was adopted unanimously. The U.S. representative then introduced additional legal and pragmatic points to convince the Council that the OAS should handle the case. Lodge, apparently ignoring the prior French resolution that confirmed the Council's jurisdiction, succeeded in mustering enough votes to prevent adoption of the agenda, thereby turning the question over to the OAS. The American government's maneuver, aimed at preventing further Soviet exploitation of the Guatemalan disorders for propaganda purposes, succeeded. On July 9, 1954, the Guatemalan government informed the Council of the restoration of order in the country.

Hungary

In the aftermath of the Suez crisis, the Hungarian revolution of 1956 came to the Council under Article 34. The Soviet Union, charged in a U.S. draft resolution with using its troops against the Hungarian nation in violation of Article 2:4, sought to prevent U.N. action on the disorder. The Soviets persistently defended their behavior as legitimate under Article 2:7 and provisions of the Warsaw Treaty. The Soviet military intervention in Hungary succeeded in quelling the uprising within the space of a few days. Russian vetoes frustrated effective Council treatment of the rebellion until its outcome was irreversible, but the critical factor in the outcome of the Hungarian case was the unwillingness of the United States to risk national or international intervention in an area of direct Soviet control.

The United States, after defeat of its draft resolution

calling for the withdrawal of Soviet forces from Hungary, submitted another draft resolution calling for a special session of the Assembly under the Uniting for Peace Resolution. The subsequent resolutions of the Assembly,[14] in addition to calling for the withdrawal of Soviet forces, expressed the concern of the Organization for the plight of refugees and authorized the dispatch of observers to the scene to report via the Secretary-General on the situation created by foreign intervention in Hungary.

On January 10, 1957, after continued Soviet noncompliance with prior U.N. resolutions, the Assembly adopted a resolution establishing a United Nations Special Committee on the Problem of Hungary.[15] The Special Committee, which included representatives of Australia, Ceylon, Denmark, Tunisia, and Uruguay, held interviews with refugees in the major European capitals. The Hungarian government, with Soviet backing, consistently refused the Special Committee entrance to the country. The report of the Special Committee to the Assembly stressed the total lack of cooperation of the Kadar regime.[16] The Special Committee found that Soviet terror had suppressed a spontaneous uprising, and that in view of the extensive foreign intervention in the Hungarian internal strife, U.N. consideration of the disorder was legally permissible. The Assembly endorsed the report and in its thirteenth session considered additional reports—one from its Special Representative on the Hungarian Problem.

[14] General Assembly Resolutions 1005 and 1006 (ES-II), November 9, 1956; 1127 (XI) and 1131 (XI), November 21 and December 12, 1956.
[15] General Assembly Resolution 1132 (XI), January 10, 1957.
[16] U.N. Doc. A/3592, June 12, 1957.

In subsequent years, Sir Leslie Munro, appointed as U.N. Special Representative, submitted a series of reports corroborating the Special Committee's findings that the U.S.S.R. had deprived Hungary of its liberty and political independence; Sir Leslie also accused the Hungarian government of engaging in execution and deportation of leaders of anti-government factions. Additional Assembly resolutions decried the "illegal actions" of the Soviet Union. The propaganda value to Western countries of continuing investigation kept the Hungarian question before the Assembly long after the outcome of the conflict was irreversible. Sir Leslie's activities were finally terminated in 1963 when the U.S. and the U.S.S.R. agreed that maintaining the Hungarian question on the Assembly's agenda would not serve a useful purpose. Not only had the propaganda value of the item diminished as newer issues occupied the Assembly, but the more cordial atmosphere obtaining between the superpowers made retention of the question and further reports unnecessary.

Lebanon

U.N. investigations in the Greek and Hungarian disorders were fact-finding endeavors that permitted the Western states and others to inquire into events alleged, in Council complaints, to have taken place in order to corroborate or disprove charges of external aggression or subversion in internal conflicts. Another opportunity for U.N. inquiry into alleged external interference in internal disturbances arose in 1958 when Lebanon, in a communication to the Council, charged that the U.A.R. was interfering in Lebanese internal affairs by supplying arms to rebels and broadcasting incendiary propaganda against the Chamoun regime. The U.A.R. asserted that President Chamoun's desire for a second term had sparked the disturbance. The Council responded to Lebanon's charge with passage of a Swedish draft resolution establishing an observer group "to proceed to Lebanon so as to ensure that there is no illegal infiltration of personnel or supply of arms or other matériel across the Lebanese borders."[17] The functions of the observer group, when proposed, were regarded by at least one delegation as distinguishable from those of U.N. investigation committees. The Panamanian representative expressed the view that

> an observation group would not have the authority to undertake an inquiry into causes and past incidents to find out whether such infiltration has already taken place. This is the essential distinction between an observation committee and a committee of investigation. An observation committee is concerned with observation of future events. An investigatory committee is concerned with discovering the truth about what has happened. . . . Clearly, in the present case, it is not the intention to create an instrument to carry out an investigation in accordance with Article 34. To give it such powers [power to investigate into events prior to its constitution] would create a situation which would lead to charges and counter-charges, thus widening the area of disagreement.[18]

Pursuant to the Council's resolution, three observers, with supporting staff, were sent to the scene; they re-

---

[17] Security Council Resolution S/4023, June 11, 1958.
[18] Security Council, *Official Records*, Thirteenth Year, 825th Meeting (June 11, 1958), p. 3.

ported that the vast majority of armed men observed were Lebanese nationals and not infiltrators. Four additional reports confirmed the initial conclusion, despite the Lebanese government's denial.[19] After the Iraqi government's overthrow in July 1958 the United States landed marines in Lebanon at President Chamoun's request. The Swedish representative, whose government had proposed the first observer group, rejected the American view that its action fell within the meaning of Article 51 and argued that in the altered circumstances UNOGIL should be suspended. The U.S. favored extension rather than termination of the Observation Group. Members of UNOGIL proposed an increase in size to 200 persons so that direct patrolling of the frontier could be facilitated. After Soviet, Swedish, and American draft resolutions were defeated, an emergency session of the Assembly was called in August 1958.

On August 21st, a draft resolution proposed by ten Arab states was adopted. The Assembly resolution called upon the Secretary-General to facilitate the withdrawal of foreign troops from Lebanon and Jordan and upon governments to refrain from interfering in the internal affairs of other states.[20] UNOGIL was expanded in size under the Secretary-General's direction and then terminated in December 1958, after the officials of Lebanon and the U.A.R. had informed the Council of the restoration of normal relations between them and the withdrawal of American troops from Lebanon and British forces from Jordan.

[19] See U.N. Docs. S/4040 and Corr. 1 and Add. 1, July 3, 1958; S/4069, July 30, 1958; S/4085, August 14, 1958; S/4100, September 20, 1958; and S/4114, November 17, 1958.
[20] General Assembly Resolution 1237 (ES-III), August 21, 1958.

Yemen

An occasion to apply techniques developed in the United Nations' involvement in Lebanon arose in connection with the Yemen civil war in 1963. From its beginnings in 1962 the Yemen internal conflict developed as a proxy war. Nasser's attempt to align the small republic with the U.A.R. is an integral part of his plan to eliminate British influence in the region. But his support of the rebels who drove the ruling Imam from power has been matched by Saudi Arabia's assistance to Yemen royalist guerrillas. With Nasser's military and political aid, Marshal Sallal established a republican regime in Yemen, a regime recognized by the United States in late December 1962. The United States favored some form of U.N. participation in a political solution, participation that would neither tax the resources of the Organization nor tarnish its prestige, in view of the mounting difficulties attending U.N. involvement in the Congo.

Two missions, one undertaken by Ellsworth Bunker for the United States and one by Ralph Bunche for the United Nations, preceded formal Council consideration of the Yemen question.[21] The prior negotiations between the Secretary-General and the governments of Saudi Arabia, the U.A.R., and the Yemen Arab Republic on terms of disengagement and a demilitarized zone continued while the Council debated the organization and mandate of the proposed observer corps.[22] Mindful of the need to avoid the financial pitfalls of ONUC, U

[21] See U.N. Docs. S/5298, April 29, 1963; S/5321, May 27, 1963; S/5323, June 3, 1963; and S/5325, June 7, 1963.

[22] See Security Council, *Official Records,* Eighteenth Year, 1037th-1039th Meetings (June 10-11, 1963).

Thant had persuaded the U.A.R. and Saudi Arabia to pay the estimated costs of UNYOM for two months' time. A joint draft resolution sponsored by Ghana and Morocco was adopted with Soviet abstention. The resolution represented a compromise between the Soviet insistence on an explicit statement of the operation's duration and financing and the British-American desire to avoid the implication that dispatch of the mission was conditional on payment by the parties concerned. The Council conferred responsibility for the corps on the Secretary-General, and for the first time in a resolution included detailed references to financing.[23] Indicating a cautious approach, Brazil and the Philippines insisted that the situation in Yemen and the Council's resolution were both *sui generis* and that the resolution could not be regarded as establishing a precedent for the future.[24]

In extending UNYOM's mandate beyond the first, second, and third two-month periods, the Council affirmed that the observers should in no way interfere in Yemen's internal affairs. During its fourteen-month existence, UNYOM reported the movement of troops and other developments of military significance,[25] but the observation corps in no way prevented the armed insurrection from persisting with external support. When the mission was terminated in September 1964, it was not certain that interested parties would agree to fruitful negotiations on Yemen's future status as an independent state.

[23] Security Council Resolution S/5330, June 11, 1963.

[24] Security Council, *Official Records*, Eighteenth Year, 1039th Meeting (June 11, 1963), paras. 27 and 32.

[25] See U.N. Docs. S/5412, September 4, 1963; S/5447 and Add. 1 and 2, October 28, 31, and November 11, 1963; S/5501 and Add. 1, January 2, 1964; S/5572, March 3, 1964; S/5681, May 3, 1964; S/5794, July 2, 1964; S/5927, September 2, 1964.

Frictions had developed within the Republican regime, already torn by religious tensions, over the announced plans of Nasser and Faisal to seek a political solution to the Yemeni civil war. Republican leaders were reported to fear that a new coalition government would be offered as a compromise formula, a government to include the Imam, whom they oppose.

In Yemen the United Nations undertook small-scale observation with a view toward clarifying the factual situation and creating a climate in which negotiations among interested parties could take place. Thant's reports throughout UNYOM's mandate stressed the United Nations' extremely limited role. Responsibility for costs and for a political solution devolved squarely upon Egypt and Saudi Arabia, not upon the Organization. In Yemen, as in Lebanon, the Organization had to deal with charges of external interference in internal affairs. But UNYOM's activities took place in the context of a protracted proxy war whose character was acknowledged by all participants and third parties. Clearly the strictly limited nature of UNYOM was shaped by the Congo experience as well as by the particular qualities of the Yemen civil war.

The intransigence of Egyptian and Saudi Arabian leaders persisted in the months following UNYOM's termination. Egypt continued to maintain a large military establishment in Yemen; the war itself continued to dislocate economic life in the country. In July 1965 a military regime replaced the civilian Republican administration of Ahmed Noman, who had sought to effect a withdrawal of Egyptian forces and to foster amicable relations with Saudi Arabia. In August, an agreement between Yemeni tribal chiefs to end the civil war was announced. The agreement, followed by an accord between Nasser and Faisal, called for the withdrawal of Egyptian forces and the formation of a Moslem state to be governed by a temporary presidential council assisted by an advisory council. A plebiscite to determine the attitude of the population toward a monarchy, a republic, or an imamate was promised.[26]

In the year following the improvement of relations between Egypt and Saudi Arabia, the number of Egyptian forces in Yemen was reportedly reduced, yet the remaining troops attempted to consolidate their hold on the country. A political solution adhered to by all parties appeared remote as an atmosphere of stalemate continued. The Egyptian-sponsored coup in Yemen in September 1966 further diminished the chances for a negotiated settlement.

Indochina

A role more limited than that played by the Organization in the Yemen proxy war has characterized its involvement in the series of internal conflicts in the former Indochina. These conflicts, waged by indigenous groups and major powers in the context first of colonial wars and later of proxy wars, have found French and American political leaders choosing to meet insurgency in the region with military responses, excluding extensive U.N. participation. French officials, attempting to restore authority in the region after World War II, showed no enthusiasm for recourse to the United Nations. They regarded French interests in Indochina as exclusively national. The Security Council's evident paralysis in East-West issues, coupled with the treat-

[26] The *New York Times*, August 14, 1965.

ment accorded the Netherlands in the Indonesian case, did not suggest that other member-states would regard the restoration of French authority as the necessary or preferable outcome of the colonial war being waged against the European power in Southeast Asia. After the Korean War, Britain and the United States, as French allies and permanent members of the Council, opposed discussion within the Organization, fearing an invitation to Russian interference in the region and unwelcome pressures to commit their own resources more heavily against Communist intrusion. The insurgents, receiving external aid from Communist sources, were achieving the result they desired without need of formal international structures. The U.S. entry into the post-Dienbienphu vacuum after the French defeat decreased the chances for immediate U.N. engagement. American disillusionment with the military and political stalemate in Korea suggested that if the United States did become involved in future proxy wars in states along the Asian power frontier these conflicts would be handled outside the Organization.

In the years following 1954 the United States elected to combat the Communist thrust in Laos and Vietnam with gradations of military and economic assistance, negotiated settlements outside the United Nations, and diplomatic backing for coalition regimes. Due to the nature of these conflicts, the United States has regarded its own power as the most reliable instrument for confronting Communist created or abetted insurgency in Southeast Asia, but it did support the establishment of an investigatory sub-committee for Laos in 1959. The Laotian government had sent an urgent appeal requesting the Secretary-General to convene the Security

Council in emergency session with a view toward the dispatch of a peace-keeping force. The commitments of both the superpowers to various factions in the internal conflict were known when the Laotian request was submitted. When the Council established the sub-committee, over Soviet protest, it empowered it "to examine the statements made before the Security Council concerning Laos, to receive further statements and documents as it may determine to be necessary and to report to the Security Council as soon as possible."[27] The sub-committee, composed of representatives from Argentina, Italy, Japan, and Tunisia, visited Laos between September 15th and October 15th. The group confined itself to fact-finding and excluded recommendations from its report. The investigators carefully sidestepped the controversial issues posed by the original Laotian complaint—the alleged aggression from North Vietnam. The final report denied claims that Vietnamese forces had staged an invasion of Laos, although their acts of infiltration were acknowledged. The report contained no conclusions on the admissibility of these actions and no suggestions for future U.N. steps in the conflict.[28]

In subsequent years, the minor role of the United Nations has continued despite the more extensive third-party participation in the region's continuing disorders. The notorious instabilities of the Laotian and Viet-

[27] Security Council Resolution S/4126, September 7, 1959. The Soviet representative had argued that the draft resolution was a substantive matter, but by a vote of 10-1, the Council adopted the resolution as procedural and hence not subject to the veto.

[28] U.N. Doc. S/4236, November 5, 1959. The Council took no further action, but the Secretary-General, in an independent capacity, visited Laos and later received a report on the economic needs of the country from Sakari Tuomioja. Tuomioja's recommendations were then discussed by the United Nations Commissioner for technical assistance and Laotian officials.

namese governmental authorities (the collapse of the 1962 coalition in Laos and the successive coups in South Vietnam) have reinforced the reluctance of America's allies to augment U.S. aid to the two states with regionally derived economic or military assistance. Neither SEATO nor NATO has played a significant part in the American actions. Again in 1963, the United Nations made an insignificant contribution to easing tensions in the region when a fact-finding group sent to South Vietnam interviewed governmental authorities, religious leaders, and students in connection with alleged violations of human rights against the Buddhists on the part of the Diem government. Members of the political opposition were not interviewed. The group's report[29] contained no conclusions, and by the time it was submitted to the Organization a coup had unseated Diem and religious persecution had ceased to be an issue.

In mid-1964, increased guerrilla activity in Laos and Vietnam led some statesmen to consider the possibility of a U.N. role in the interrelated internal conflicts in the former Indochinese states, a role that might exceed investigation. On May 13, 1964, the Cambodian government requested a meeting of the Security Council to consider its charges that the armed forces of the United States and the Republic of Vietnam had committed aggressive acts against Cambodian territory. The Cambodian representative asked that a U.N. mission of inquiry be established to investigate these acts and that the 1954 Geneva Conference be reconvened in order to guarantee Cambodian neutrality and territorial integrity, thus facilitating the work of the International

[29] U.N. Doc. A/5630, December 7, 1963.

Control Commission[30] in monitoring the border between Cambodia and Vietnam.

The U.S. delegate, in denying the charges against his government, stated the willingness of American authorities to consider proposals for U.N. machinery to help stabilize frontier conditions between Cambodia and South Vietnam. Similarly, the Vietnam observer at the United Nations denied that his country had committed aggressive acts against Cambodia. After the Soviet representative denounced the U.S. military involvement in Southeast Asia, the U.S. delegate expressed the view that the idea of a border patrol reporting to the Secretary-General augmented by U.N. observers under a U.N. command should be considered.[31]

After a recess in debate, the Council reconvened and unanimously adopted a resolution representing a compromise of conflicting interests. Taking note of the incidents complained of by Cambodia, the Council's resolution established a three-man mission to investigate Cambodian charges.[32] In presenting the draft resolution, the Moroccan representative stressed that its sponsors wished to deal only with the Cambodian complaint, not with the general problem of instability in Southeast Asia.[33] The American representative asked that the

[30] The International Control Commissions for Supervision and Control in Vietnam, Laos, and Cambodia were established in 1954 to supervise the execution of the Geneva cease-fire agreements that stopped the fighting between the French and the Vietminh on the Indochinese peninsula. They are not agents of the United Nations; they were set up by Britain and the Soviet Union, co-chairmen of the conference, in order to assist in bringing the hostilities to an orderly conclusion.

[31] Security Council, *Official Records*, Nineteenth Year, 1119th Meeting (May 21, 1964), paras. 75-77.

[32] Security Council Resolution S/5741, June 4, 1964.

[33] Security Council, *Official Records*, Nineteenth Year, 1126th Meeting (June 4, 1964), paras. 3-10.

Commission consider the broader purposes of U.N. peace-keeping when submitting its report.[34]

On July 27, 1964, the representatives of Morocco, the Ivory Coast, and Brazil, who undertook the mission, submitted a report favoring some form of continuing U.N. presence in the area.[35] The participating members stated that a restoration of political relations between Cambodia and the Republic of Vietnam, made difficult by ancient rivalries and contemporary distrust, would be desirable as a prelude to eventual agreements on the delimitation and marking of the frontier. The members of the mission recommended that the Security Council should consider the possibility of establishing a U.N. observer group with functions to include supervision in the frontier area. The recommendation has not been implemented by the Council.

The 1964 phase of diplomatic intercourse was significant for the widespread questioning of the post-Korea assumption that the United Nations could contribute nothing to the solution of Asian proxy wars involving the major powers. Thant, revising an earlier estimation that the Organization should play no role in any phase of the Indochinese conflicts,[36] stated that the United Nations' resources would permit international supervision of any political settlement interested states, members and non-members, might negotiate.[37] In February 1965, after the United States' retaliatory air strikes on North Vietnamese territory, Thant couched his appeal for negotiations to include all principal parties in terms precluding an extensive role for the Organization:

[34] *Ibid.*, paras. 54-59.
[35] U.N. Doc. S/5832, July 27, 1964.
[36] The *New York Times*, March 3, 1964.
[37] *Ibid.*, July 7, 1964.

I am greatly disturbed by recent events in Southeast Asia, and particularly by the seriously deteriorating situation in Vietnam. My fear, frankly, is in regard to the dangerous possibilities of escalation, because such a situation, if it should once get out of control, would obviously pose the gravest threat to the peace of the world. . . .

I am conscious of course of my responsibilities under Article 99 of the Charter. I am also aware that there are many difficulties in the way of attempting a United Nations solution to the problem, in view of its past history and the fact that some of the principal parties are not represented in the United Nations.[38]

The steady extension of the Vietnam war after the start of American bombing of the North has served to keep open the issue of U.N. participation in the conflict.

The U.S. government in its letter of August 1, 1965,[39] brought the Vietnam conflict to the Council's attention. The letter did not request a formal Council meeting, nor did the American gesture toward the Organization signify that U.S. officials were preparing to place less emphasis on their military efforts in North and South Vietnam. The U.S. request that member-states assist in finding a solution to the conflict could not be construed as an indication that the Johnson administration regarded the resources of the United Nations as a possible substitute for the U.S. military presence in Southeast Asia.

The American pause in bombing raids in late December 1965 and January 1966 afforded interested states

[38] *Ibid.*, February 25, 1965.
[39] U.N. Doc. S/6575, August 1, 1965.

another opportunity to furnish suggestions that might lead to negotiations. These efforts, like prior initiatives of non-permanent members of the Security Council and members of the British Commonwealth, proved fruitless. The resumption of bombing was accompanied by a surprise request for a Security Council meeting. In appealing to the Council, the U.S. government submitted a draft resolution that asked the Council to call for immediate discussions without preconditions among interested governments. The resolution, which looked toward an application of the Geneva Accords of 1954 and 1962, recommended that a new conference should regard a cessation of hostilities as a priority.[40]

A bitter debate followed Ambassador Goldberg's presentation. After lengthy arguments were heard favoring and opposing the American position, the newly enlarged Council voted to inscribe the Vietnam question on its agenda. Voting with the United States were Argentina, China, Japan, Jordan, Netherlands, New Zealand, Great Britain, and Uruguay. Bulgaria and the Soviet Union voted against inclusion of the item; France, Mali, Nigeria, and Uganda abstained. The delegates of the Soviet Union and Bulgaria decried the renewed bombing attacks on North Vietnam and accused the United States of attempting to use the Security Council as "smoke-screen" for its "barbarous" actions.[41] The French representative declared that the United Nations could not serve as the appropriate forum for achieving a peaceful solution since only one principal party, the United States, was represented in

[40] U.N. Doc. S/7106, January 31, 1966.
[41] See *U.N. Monthly Chronicle*, III (March 1966) 5.

the Organization.[42] The delegates of Mali and Uganda agreed that a Council debate would serve no useful purpose.[43] After the vote, at the suggestion of the Council's President, the delegate from Japan, the Council adjourned in order to undertake private consultations. These talks, he later reported to the Secretary-General,[44] indicated continued disagreement among the various representatives on the wisdom of Council involvement in the Vietnam question. Thus the Council remained seized of the issue, yet unable to render any effective assistance in the conflict.

In the months following the Council's debate on the Vietnam conflict, the Secretary-General, in a series of addresses and press conferences, stated his own views on the continuing threat posed to international peace and security by the war. Citing the lack of consensus among the big powers, whose endorsement would be needed for a U.N. peace-keeping role in Vietnam, U Thant reiterated his proposal for three steps that should be taken in order to create an atmosphere conducive to negotiations: cessation of the bombing of North Vietnam, the scaling down of all military operations in South Vietnam, and a willingness on the part of all parties to enter into discussion with those who are actually fighting.

U Thant's discouragement over the continuation of the Vietnam conflict figured prominently in his decision to decline a second term as Secretary-General. After numerous discussions with key delegations, he reversed his announced plans to leave the Secretariat.

[42] *Ibid.*, p. 6. [43] *Ibid.*, p. 6.
[44] U.N. Doc. S/7168, February 26, 1966. Objections to the President's letter were registered by the U.S.S.R., Bulgaria, and Mali.

In accepting a second term, Thant cited his determination to press for a peaceful solution to the Asian conflict. A new opportunity for the Secretary-General to influence the course of events developed in December 1966 when the American government, through Ambassador Goldberg, requested Thant to take "whatever steps you consider necessary to bring about the necessary discussions which could lead to . . . a cease-fire."[45] The Secretary-General, replying to the United States' letter, stated his willingness to cooperate with all parties in the search for peace on the basis of his three-point proposal.

Behind-the-scenes discussions may continue while the conflict rages. Such discussions rather than formal U.N. debates are in keeping with the nature of the Vietnam conflict and the inherent disabilities the Organization faces in coping with violence centering on the actions of the superpowers and China. Such discussions do not commit the United Nations' prestige to a particular outcome, nor do they force the Organization to align itself with one of two key permanent members of the Security Council. The efficacy of these talks is diminished when non-member-states or non-governments are primary actors in the conflict, as in the Vietnam war. When the willingness of parties to negotiate is uncertain, or when the negotiating positions of the parties are hardened in the face of escalating violence, U.N. participation may yield few positive results unless major powers give full support to the Organization's attempts. The deepened commitment of the American government to the fortunes of the Saigon regime suggests that if some form of negotiated settlement does

[45] See U.N. Doc. S/7641, December 19, 1966.

result from policy choices open to the major participants, it is unlikely that a U.N. role in such a settlement would exceed that played by the Organization in
1954 when the International Control Commission was
established, prior to direct involvement of the United
States and the Soviet Union in the region.

Conclusion

The involvement of the United States and the Soviet
Union in disorders in Greece, Guatemala, Lebanon,
Hungary, Laos, and Vietnam has given to these conflicts an international dimension and global significance.
Similarly, the participation of Egypt and Saudi Arabia
in the Yemen conflict increased the concern of other
third-party states for regional security and international
stability. In these conflicts, the Soviet Union and the
United States have sought to use the United Nations or
to preclude its participation according to the nature
of their interests. Propaganda advantages have figured
prominently in the attitudes of both superpowers toward U.N. consideration of particular cases. Thus in
Lebanon and Guatemala, the Soviet Union did not intend to intervene directly; it used the United Nations
to expose American actions it regarded as detrimental.
Similarly, the United States did not intend to intervene
directly in Hungary; it used the United Nations as a
forum for marshalling opinion against Soviet repression
in 1956 and for years thereafter.

The avoidance of a U.N. commitment to a particular
outcome has characterized the Organization's investigation and observation activities in Greece, Lebanon,
Yemen, Laos, and South Vietnam. These activities,
while serving to clarify charges and countercharges

brought to the Assembly and Council, have at best created a pause in which parties could move toward negotiations. In many instances, for example Laos or South Vietnam, the reports themselves have been of little consequence, since they have dealt with limited facets of complicated issues in a limited fashion. In other cases, as in Lebanon, Hungary, or Yemen, the findings of U.N. investigators or observers, while providing impartial information or conclusions, have made little difference to the eventual settlement of these disorders.

Like the colonial wars and internal conflicts involving a breakdown of law and order, some internal conflicts involving alleged external subversion or aggression have become protracted disorders as in Greece, Yemen, and Vietnam. But in Guatemala, Hungary, and Lebanon, violence had erupted suddenly and subsided quickly. The greater diversity of these individual conflicts distinguishes them from the colonial wars and internal conflicts involving a breakdown of law and order in which recurring patterns of interest among local parties have been discerned. A limited U.N. involvement, one entailing debate, resolution, and perhaps some form of investigation and observation, is the most significant precedent to emerge from the Organization's responses to contemporary internal conflicts involving charges of external aggression or subversion and proxy wars.

CHAPTER V

World Order and Local Disorder:
Retrospect and Prospect

SINCE 1946 the United Nations' interests in the maintenance of international peace and security and the pacific settlement of disputes have been expressed in a variety of internal conflicts revealing new conceptions of the relationship between the domestic and international order in world politics. Some conflicts touched off significant turmoil for limited periods of time, with important international ramifications, but remained isolated or contained, as in Guatemala, Greece, Lebanon, Yemen, and the Dominican Republic. Some internal disorders have confronted the Organization with the need to assist in the conception of political solutions when other formulas have proved unworkable, as in Indonesia and Cyprus. Others have required the Organization to assume a major role in containing internal violence and preventing external interventions, as in the Congo. The United Nations has performed different functions—investigating, observing, and keeping-the-peace—in different internal conflicts, and has played different roles at different times in its history. The efficacy of its procedures has varied with the type of internal conflict the Organization has attempted to resolve in each case.

The United Nations' responses to internal conflicts have been characterized by limited means and limited achievements. The U.N. record in colonial wars, internal disorders involving a breakdown of law and order or charges of subversion or external aggression, and proxy wars contains examples of "pacific non-settlement" and "not-quite-pacific settlement."[1] The disorders studied in Chapters 2, 3, and 4 indicate the extent to which local parties to internal conflicts and their foreign supporters are capable of resisting U.N. appeals or pressures for peaceful change, for an end to violence, for the protection of human rights. The cumulative compromises that have marked the Organization's responses to differing internal conflicts are evidence that the United Nations remains closely tied to the political environment.

The reasons why the Organization has become involved in internal conflicts have varied from case to case, just as the types of conflict themselves have exhibited varying characteristics. In the recent colonial conflicts, notably Angola, the Organization has become involved not only because of the presumed threat to international peace and security but because of the present majority's concern with all aspects of colonialism. The non-colonial internal conflicts do not present a similar picture. It is the violence of these individual outbreaks that has concerned the United Nations rather than some broad movements of which the non-colonial internal wars might be a part. The Organization's influence in conflicts directly involving the United States and the Soviet Union has continued to be negligible from Hungary through the Dominican Republic and Vietnam.

The U.N. record contains examples of items of civil disorder submitted in conformity with various motives of incumbents, insurgents, and third parties. Incumbent governments have appealed to the United Nations in

[1] Inis Claude, *Swords Into Plowshares*, 2nd ed. (New York: Random House, 1959), p. 216.

hopes of restoring order and authority, as in the Congo, or of ending foreign intervention in support of rebels, as in Cyprus, Greece, Lebanon, and Guatemala. Through the intercession of sympathetic third parties, rebels have exposed excesses of colonial regimes, as in Angola and Algeria, and obtained greater status in negotiations with incumbents, as in Indonesia. Aside from a general interest in halting violence, third parties have on occasion espoused the cause of incumbents or insurgents in order to marshal public opinion against cold-war adversaries, as in Hungary, or to condemn unilateral interventions, as in Lebanon, the Dominican Republic, and Vietnam.

Whether or not incumbents, insurgents, and third parties have favored U.N. participation in a particular conflict has depended in part on the prior responses of the Organization to similar disturbances and the likelihood of interference with bilateral or regional negotiations pending or in progress. In addition, incumbents, insurgents, and third parties have had to consider whether the United Nations could be used to facilitate a lasting solution to the conflict or merely to restore a disadvantageous status quo, and whether the ad hoc paramilitary forces of interposition the Organization might be able to field would be adequate for terminating hostilities. These considerations may become more consequential in the coming decade if patterns of violence in the political environment assume the characteristics suggested by Samuel Huntington:

> Most violence will be civil violence in that it occurs within the accepted boundaries of particular political units. All violence will be civil violence in that it oc-

curs within the great society of world politics in which almost all nations and governments recognize a common interest in minimizing intergovernmental war and in which domestic violence in one country resembles and is influenced by patterns of violence in other countries belonging to the same transnational political community.[2]

While third-party states with national political interests in internal violence cannot be expected to forego chances for securing favorable outcomes via bilateral, regional, or multilateral means, the alternatives of anarchy or internal rivalries escalating into uncontrollable hostilities are not attractive options for states in a nuclear world. Thus the self-restraint of states will be a critical factor in determining whether "the great society of world politics" becomes in practice as well as in theory a "transnational political community." The role the United Nations might come to play in fostering the interests of such a community is suggested by a reconsideration of the questions investigated in the preceding chapters.[3]

The interests of the United Nations in internal disorders judged to threaten international peace and security have remained constant from the postwar disturbances in Greece and Indonesia through the more recent conflicts in Cyprus and the Dominican Republic. It has become more difficult for the Organization to realize these interests in its second decade. The national interests of the Soviet Union, China, the United States, and others in intrastate violence have intensified

[2] Samuel P. Huntington (ed.), *Changing Patterns of Military Politics* (New York: Free Press of Glencoe, 1962), p. 47.
[3] See Introduction, p. 8.

since 1955. During the same period, especially from 1960 onward, the Organization has progressed toward universality. The entry of the newly independent African states has brought extensive problems of internal disorder to the attention of both the General Assembly and the Security Council and has deepened the commitment of the Organization to change. In the colonial and post-colonial disorders, the European powers associated with a political and economic status quo have been placed on the defensive before the United Nations' political organs. The influx of former colonies and other new states into the Organization has also made achievement of the consensus necessary for U.N. actions in internal disorders, as in other conflicts, a more complex process.

The newer nations' concern for self-determination, for racial equality, and for social and economic development has focussed the continuing attention of the Organization on the process of decolonization. The majority of states has favored a transfer of power to indigenous groups rather than recognition of the legitimacy of the colonial powers' prewar authority. The post-colonial phase, in which world order is threatened by a proliferation of unviable states susceptible to competitive big-power influences or interventions and to intercommunal tensions, has occupied the Organization since the Congo's first days of independence. The United Nations has attempted to restore order, to work for political reconciliation, to prevent national interventions from widening the area of conflict when intrastate violence has erupted. While the Organization has adopted a consistent approach, the post-colonial breakdowns of law and order in the Congo and Cyprus became protracted conflicts, revealing a lack of the national consensus needed for peaceful self-rule. The majority of states favored solutions that would preserve these states from division into smaller political units with still greater vulnerability to outside penetration or economic collapse. The claims of "self-determination" by parts of these new states, for example, Katanga and the Turkish Cypriot minority, have been rejected in favor of strengthening the legitimacy of incumbent regimes.

In the three types of internal disorders examined, founding and newer members have displayed a common reluctance to endorse advance obligations for themselves or for the Organization. Political and, to a lesser extent, legal factors have influenced the choice of procedures adopted. In internal conflicts like the Algerian and Vietnam wars, conflicts from which some permanent members of the Security Council have wished to exclude the Organization, the United Nations has expressed its concern in limited responses, including discussion or passage of innocuous resolutions, or has taken no action. In cases in which consensus has permitted a more extensive response, where a majority of states has approved the expression of a U.N. interest but not commitment to a particular outcome, the Organization has established investigatory bodies and observer corps. These techniques have served a variety of purposes for member-states, ranging from fact-finding to propaganda. The Organization has conducted various types of investigations in different kinds of internal disorders with similar results; external political factors have been important in determining the outcome of internal conflicts the United Nations has investigated. In Greece, Hungary, and Laos the interests of

Western states seeking to use the United Nations as a forum for exposing Communist subversion and manipulation of internal conflicts were served. The Organization by means of its investigatory role expressed an interest when no stronger U.N. action was possible. In Angola, U.N. investigation has yielded information for African states and others seeking to force Portugal's compliance with Council and Assembly resolutions. In Greece, Hungary, Laos, and Angola, reports of subsidiary bodies established to inquire into charges or countercharges served to substantiate or refute claims of wrongdoing without committing the Organization to an interventionary role. These reports might carry greater weight if the United Nations were to have at its disposal a permanent corps of officials or rapporteurs to perform investigating services so that the political organs could deal with corroborated claims of disputants. A similar corps of mediators would facilitate the Organization's work in aiding negotiations between parties.[4]

Like the technique of investigation, the technique of observation has permitted the United Nations to express a concern in a particular disorder when, as in the Yemen and Lebanon conflicts, external political factors have precluded stronger interposition. Of limited value, observation is also of limited risk for the Organization and is therefore likely to retain its utility as a method of pacific settlement in conformity with the United Nations' purposes and principles. Such approaches to pacific settlement do not entail great political or financial risks for the United Nations as do peace-keeping operations undertaken in circumstances of internal

[4] For a fuller exposition of these proposals, see Benjamin V. Cohen, "Using the United Nations," *The New Republic*, May 8, 1965, pp. 13-16.

strife. As the analysis of ONUC and UNFICYP clarified, the risks of peace-keeping may be greater in an internal conflict than in an interstate dispute. The peace-keeping force itself may become a stake in big-power competition, or an expensive drain on the Organization's financial resources and prestige. It may carry out its vague mandates only by calling its presumed non-interventionary character into question. Investigation and observation are thus alternatives for the Organization if the membership wishes to express an interest, but not necessarily a commitment, in a particular internal disorder.

The United Nations has expressed its concern for the outcome of several internal conflicts in collective actions requiring a prolonged consensus. Some collective actions, such as the arms embargo in the Angolan case, have placed on it no financial or political burdens, but their effectiveness has been negligible. In the Indonesian case, consensus between the United States and the U.S.S.R., in marked contrast to their positions in the later Indochinese internal conflicts, allowed the Organization to contribute to the containment of local violence through its efforts at arranging cease-fires and other field activities, and through its resolutions urging a peaceful settlement and transfer of governmental power. The Congo and Cyprus peace-keeping operations represent the United Nations' deepest commitment, as well as expression of concern, in internal conflicts. The breakdown of the initial Soviet-American consensus and the series of splits within the African group of states embroiled the Secretariat in disputes with third parties pressing for outcomes favorable to their own interests and hindered the Congo field operation. Logistical problems and politically inspired financial and constitutional difficulties called the efficacy of the Organization's protracted collective action into question. The more stable consensus in the Cyprus conflict has been achieved by setting limits to U.N. action, by imposing time and cost restrictions on the field mission, by placing the burden for political settlement on the parties themselves rather than upon the Organization. A consensus has enabled UNFICYP to function, but only with an unclear mandate, especially with regard to its use of arms, and a small force-in-being.

The Charter, as a legal basis for international control of internal conflict, has served as a flexible instrument for actions the majority of states at a given moment in the Organization's history has supported—investigation, observation, or peace-keeping operations looking toward peaceful settlement. The Organization's approach to internal disorders, an approach in which the legal basis for U.N. action is often unclear, attests to the presence of ad hoc political majorities. These majorities have produced resolutions increasingly couched in ambiguous language without citation of Charter articles, resolutions deliberately structured to avoid establishing precedents. Delegates have used or discarded Charter labels or blurred distinctions between Charter articles, especially those in Chapters VI and VII, depending upon whether the language of relevant articles has appeared to fit their interpretations of a particular conflict. Nevertheless, significant trends of Charter usage and interpretation have developed in U.N. practice. States who have wished to block discussion or action in specific conflicts have relied heavily on the domestic jurisdiction principle, while states who have advocated U.N. resolutions have insisted that the situation at hand has constituted a threat to international peace and security under Article 39. In domestic disorders involving human rights, states have augmented the Article 2:7 argument with claims that Articles 55 and 56 are statements of intent and do not constitute "legal obligations" binding on members. In internal disorders involving allegations of subversion or indirect aggression, members have drafted their statements in the language of Article 39, and have on occasion added charges of external aggression in violation of Article 2:4. The majority of member-states has consistently rejected readings of Article 2:7 that would limit the Organization's capacity to realize its major purpose—the maintenance of international peace and security. At the same time, Article 39 has been used as an elastic provision, one enabling the United Nations to consider a wide range of colonial, post-colonial, and other intrastate disorders.

The Council's avoidance of the use of Articles 41 and 42 in responding to threats to peace posed by internal violence constitutes another significant trend of Charter usage and interpretation. Practically, policy differences and the lack of a permanent stand-by force have militated against U.N. enforcement measures. Theoretically, internal conflicts have posed the question, Enforcement against whom? Against the rebelling faction, the host state, or legitimate government? Against interested parties who may be former colonial administrators? Defining "enforcement measures" in the context of relations between the United Nations and regional organizations has assumed added importance in the light of the OAS peace-keeping role in the Dominican Republic. Prior to the establishment of the

Inter-American Force, no regional organization had fielded a significant military force in circumstances of civil strife; a previous attempt to form a NATO force for the internal conflict in Cyprus had failed. Generally, the regional organizations, encouraged by the Charter to resolve disputes within their areas, have not played consequential roles in the resolution of intrastate violence. In some disorders of global magnitude, like the Vietnam war, the existence of regional security pacts has not resulted in regional commitments to a particular course of action. Member-states, in paying lip service to NATO or SEATO, have not adopted uniform policies in that conflict. In the Congo disorders, the OAU served as a channel for the exchange of views and the promotion of negotiations between opposing factions, but internal dissension prevented the African organization from exerting greater influence on the course of events.

The compromise in the Charter whereby regional organizations are acknowledged as institutions compatible with the United Nations' purposes and principles provides that no "enforcement action" can be taken by these groups of states without Security Council authorization. Since what constitutes "enforcement action" has not been defined, states have advanced various views to support policy positions adopted. The United States, desiring to exert maximum influence in the Western Hemisphere bilaterally and via the OAS, did not characterize its or the regional organization's actions in the Dominican Republic as "enforcement." It may be assumed that the United States would not wish to grant similar authority to other regional organizations in which it does not exercise a dominant voice. Secretary Thant, without defining enforcement action, warned of the dangers that could result for the United Nations if the OAS, the OAU, or the Arab League were to declare themselves competent to undertake enforcement action in their regions.[5] Despite its diplomatic character, the timing of Thant's statement could only suggest that the Secretary-General had misgivings about the OAS activities in the Dominican Republic.

In Richard Falk's view, the OAS intervention, as a regional intervention, should enjoy a more favorable legal status than the unilateral American intervention that preceded it. Of still greater legal authority, Falk argues, are U.N. interventions. The legitimacy of a particular intervention should be based on whether it rested on prior principles that express "patterns of general community consent or merely reflect ad hoc political majorities of the moment." Falk would give to the United Nations greater legislative competence to intervene in domestic affairs, authority that would enable the Organization to move into *any* civil disorder threatening world peace or abusing human rights. Falk asserts that when the objectives of an internal conflict express the "preferences of the world community," as in Angola or Algeria, the outcome of strife is a matter of international concern. He concludes that a world community that favors the end of colonialism and racism should not stand aloof while violence works itself out. In some instances Falk suggests that the United Na-

[5] Address of the Secretary-General to Non-Governmental Organizations, May 27, 1965, reprinted in *U.N. Monthly Chronicle*, June 1965, pp. 68-70.

tions might become the sole authority in modernizing countries experiencing civil upheaval.[6]

These suggestions are grounded in a view of world order that places highest value on the development of "community-authorized norms" to be expressed through the United Nations. The analysis presented in Chapters 1-4 has served to clarify the numerous obstacles to such a development. The universality of the Organization is incomplete. Internal conflicts occupy such a prominent place in the series of competitions between Western and Eastern groupings of states that acquiescence in a proposal to confer additional legislative responsibilities on the United Nations is unlikely. The "preferences of the world community" expressed in U.N. debates may in fact represent priorities of a vocal group of states whose influence within the Organization is disproportionate to the power they are able to wield on an individual basis outside the United Nations. The Organization in its present stage of development serves the international society, but that society is not yet an international community.

The study of the United Nations and internal disorders suggests that the diversity of contemporary internal conflicts precludes the development of general rules for its treatment of civil strife. The Organization may have a role without a rule, yet "crises need not be postponed or jeopardized merely to give the United Nations a 'role' or to build its record."[7] Not all internal conflicts need come to the Organization; whenever all parties, whatever their legal status, are encouraged to

---

[6] See Richard A. Falk, in Stanger, pp. 40-44.

[7] Louis Henkin, "The United Nations and its Supporters," *Political Science Quarterly*, LXXVIII (December 1963), 514-515.

negotiate, whether in regional contexts or via bilateral pressures, the interests of the larger international society are served.

Containment of lower levels of coercion and violence pursuant to the maintenance of international peace and security emerged as a critical problem for the United Nations in its first two decades. The importance of colonial wars has declined with grants of independence to territories. But breakdowns of law and order, proxy wars, and externally abetted or controlled internal violence may be expected to mark the United Nations' third decade. These disorders, occurring with frequency in countries whose primary needs include political, social, and economic modernization, create threats to global as well as regional order. The role the United Nations will play in the resolution of these conflicts will thus depend in large part on the attitudes of the United States and the Western states toward using the Organization as an institution for modernization. For, as Cyril Black warns,

> the best chance for a stable world today lies in . . . efforts to encourage modernization with a minimum of violence; and only those that can meet this challenge successfully can hope to see their institutions and values prevail in the emerging world.[8]

[8] Cyril E. Black, in Black and Thornton, p. 448.

Bibliography
and Index

Bibliography

The following bibliography is intended as a selective rather than exhaustive listing of relevant literature.

United Nations Official Records

Texts of General Assembly and Security Council debates are available in General Assembly, *Official Records*, and Security Council, *Official Records*. Cited reports of the Secretary-General, U.N. sub-committees and commissions, or officials of U.N. peace-keeping operations are available in collections of *United Nations Documents*. These publications may be consulted in depository libraries.

Other Materials on the United Nations

Official summaries and other information on the work of the United Nations political organs are available in the *United Nations Yearbook*, the *United Nations Review* and its successor publication, *U.N. Monthly Chronicle*. A survey is presented in "Issues Before the General Assembly," the annual fall issue of *International Conciliation*, published by the Carnegie Endowment for International Peace. Summaries of the activities of U.N. organs are also published in *International Organization*, a quarterly issued by the World Peace Foundation.

Selected Books, Monographs, and Articles

Adams, T. W., and A. J. Cottrell. "The Cyprus Conflict," *Orbis*, viii (Spring 1964), 66-83.

Alger, Chadwick F. "Non-Resolution Consequences of the United Nations and Their Effect on International Conflict," *Journal of Conflict-Resolution*, v (June 1961), 128-222.

Almond, Gabriel, and James Coleman. *The Politics of the Developing Areas*. Princeton: Princeton University Press, 1960.

Anabtawi, Samir. "The Afro-Asian States and the Hungarian Question," *International Organization*, xvii (Autumn 1963), 872-900.

Angola: Views of a Revolt. London: Oxford University Press, 1962.

Bailey, Sydney. *The General Assembly.* New York: Praeger, 1960.

―――. *The Secretariat of the United Nations.* New York: Carnegie Endowment for International Peace, 1962.

―――. *The United Nations, A Short Political Guide.* New York: Praeger, 1963.

Barnett, A. Doak. *Communist China and Asia.* New York: Random House, 1960.

Black, Cyril E., and Thomas P. Thornton (eds.). *Communism and Revolution.* Princeton: Princeton University Press, 1964.

Bloomfield, Lincoln. *The United Nations and U.S. Foreign Policy.* Boston: Little, Brown and Company, 1960.

―――. "Peacekeeping and Peacemaking," *Foreign Affairs,* xLIV (April 1966), 671-683.

Bloomfield, Lincoln, *et al. International Military Forces.* Boston: Little, Brown and Company, 1964.

Boutros-Ghali, Boutros. "The Addis Ababa Charter," *International Conciliation,* No. 546, January 1964.

Bowett, D. W. *United Nations Forces.* New York: Praeger, 1964.

Bowman, Edward, and James Fanning. "Logistical Problems of UNEF and ONUC," *International Organization,* xvII (Spring 1963), 355-377.

Boyd, James. "Cyprus: Episode in Peacekeeping," *International Organization,* xx (Winter 1966), 1-17.

Briggs, Herbert. *The Law of Nations.* 2nd ed. New York: Appleton-Century-Crofts, 1952.

Brownlie, Ian. *International Law and the Use of Force by States.* London: Oxford University Press, 1963.

Burns, Arthur Lee, and Heathcote, Nina. *Peace-keeping by U.N. Forces, From Suez through the Congo.* New York: Praeger, 1963.

Calvocoressi, Peter. *World Order and New States.* London: Catto and Windus, 1962.

Cohen, Benjamin. *The United Nations: Constitutional De-*

velopment, Growth and Possibilities. Cambridge: Harvard University Press, 1961.

———. "The United Nations in its Twentieth Year," *International Organization,* xx (Spring 1966), 185-207.

Collins, J. Foster. "The United Nations and Indonesia," *International Conciliation,* No. 458, March 1950.

Claude, Inis. "The OAS, the UN and the United States," *International Conciliation,* No. 547, March 1964.

———. "The Political Framework of the United Nations' Financial Problems," *International Organization,* xvII (Autumn 1963), 831-859.

———. *Power and International Relations.* New York: Random House, 1962.

———. *Swords Into Plowshares.* 2nd ed. New York: Random House, 1959.

———. "The United Nations and the Use of Force," *International Conciliation,* No. 532, March 1961.

———. "United Nations Use of Military Forces," *Journal of Conflict-Resolution,* vII (June 1963), 117-129.

Dallin, Alexander. *The Soviet Union at the U.N.* New York: Praeger, 1962.

Duffy, James. "Portugal in Africa," *Foreign Affairs,* xxxIx (April 1961), 481-493.

Eckstein, Harry (ed.). *Internal War: Problems and Approaches.* New York: Free Press of Glencoe, 1964.

Emerson, Rupert. "American Policy in Africa," *Foreign Affairs,* xL (January 1962), 303-315.

———. *From Empire to Nation.* Cambridge: Harvard University Press, 1960.

———. "Pan-Africanism," *International Organization,* xvI (Spring 1962), 275-290.

Falk, Richard A. *Law, Morality and War in the Contemporary World.* New York: Praeger, 1963.

Fawcett, J.E.S. "Intervention in International Law," Hague *Recueil des Cours,* 1961.

Ferguson, Allen. "Tactics in a Local Crisis," *Journal of Conflict-Resolution,* vII (June 1963), 130-140.

Foley, Charles. *Legacy of Strife: Cyprus from Rebellion to Civil War.* Baltimore: Penguin Books, 1964.

Foote, Wilder (ed.) *Dag Hammarskjöld, Servant of Peace.* New York: Harper and Row, 1962.

Gardner, Richard. "The Development of the United Nations Peace-Keeping Capacity," American Society of International Law *Proceedings*, 1963, pp. 224-233.

————. *In Pursuit of World Order.* New York: Praeger, 1964.

Garthoff, Raymond. "Unconventional Warfare in Communist Strategy," *Foreign Affairs*, XL (July 1962), 566-575.

Good, Robert C. "Changing Patterns of African International Relations," *American Political Science Review*, LVIII (September 1964), 632-641.

Goodrich, Leland M. "The Political Role of the Secretary-General," *International Organization*, XVI (Autumn 1962), 720-735.

————. *The United Nations.* New York: Thomas Crowell, 1959.

————. "The U.N. Security Council," *International Organization*, XII (Summer 1958), 273-287.

Goodrich, Leland M., and Edvard Hambro. *Charter of the United Nations: Commentary and Documents.* Revised ed. Boston: World Peace Foundation, 1949.

Goodrich, Leland M., and Norman Padelford (eds.). *The United Nations in the Balance.* New York: Praeger, 1965.

Goodrich, Leland M., and Anne Simons. *The United Nations and the Maintenance of International Peace and Security.* Washington: Brookings Institution, 1955.

Goodwin, Geoffrey. "The Political Role of the United Nations: Some British Views," *International Organization*, XV (Autumn 1961), 581-602.

Gordon, King. *The U.N. in the Congo.* New York: Carnegie Endowment for International Peace, 1962.

Gross, Ernest. *The United Nations: Structure for Peace.* New York: Harper and Brothers, 1962.

Gross, Franz (ed.). *The United States and the United Nations.* Norman, Oklahoma: University of Oklahoma Press, 1964.

Gross, Leo. "Expenses of the United Nations for Peace-Keeping Operations: The Advisory Opinion of the International Court of Justice," *International Organization,* xvii (Winter 1963), 1-35.

Gutteridge, William. *Armed Forces in the New States.* London: Oxford University Press, 1962.

Haekkerup, Per. "Scandinavia's Peace-Keeping Force for U.N.," *Foreign Affairs,* xlii (July 1964), 675-681.

Harris, Richard. *Independence and After: Revolution in Underdeveloped Countries.* London: Oxford University Press, 1962.

Henkin, Louis. "Force, Intervention and Neutrality in International Law," American Society of International Law *Proceedings,* 1963, pp. 147-163.

————. "The United Nations and Its Supporters: A Self-Examination," *Political Science Quarterly,* lxxviii (December 1963), 504-536.

Higgins, Rosalyn. *The Development of International Law Through the Political Organs of the United Nations.* London: Oxford University Press, 1963.

Hilsman, Roger, and Robert C. Good (eds.). *Foreign Policy in the Sixties: The Issues and the Instruments.* Baltimore: Johns Hopkins Press, 1965.

Hoffmann, Stanley. "In Search of a Thread: The U.N. in the Congo Labyrinth," *International Organization,* xvi (Spring 1962), 331-361.

Hogg, James Ferguson. "Peace-Keeping Costs and Charter Obligations—Implications of the International Court of Justice Decision on Certain Expenses of the United Nations," *Columbia Law Review,* lx (March 1962), 1230-1263.

Hoskyns, Catherine. *The Congo Since Independence.* London: Oxford University Press, 1965.

Hovet, Thomas, Jr. *Bloc Politics in the United Nations.* Cambridge: Harvard University Press, 1960.

Huntington, Samuel P. (ed.). *Changing Patterns of Military Politics.* New York: Free Press of Glencoe, 1962.

Jackson, Elmore. "The Developing Role of the Secretary-General," *International Organization,* xi (Summer 1957), 431-445.

Jacobson, Harold. "ONUC's Civilian Operations: State-

Building and State-Preserving," *World Politics*, xvii (October 1964), 75-107.

——. "The United Nations and Colonialism: A Tentative Appraisal," *International Organization*, xvi (Winter 1962), 37-56.

Jessup, Philip. *A Modern Law of Nations*. New York: The Macmillan Company, 1948.

Johnson, Chalmers A. "Civilian Loyalty and Guerrilla Conflict," *World Politics*, xv (July 1962), 646-661.

Kaplan, Morton A. (ed.). *The Revolution in World Politics*. New York: John Wiley and Sons, 1962.

Kaplan, Morton A., and Nicholas de B. Katzenbach. *The Political Foundations of International Law*. New York: John Wiley and Sons, 1961.

Karabus, Alan. "United Nations Activities in the Congo," American Society of International Law *Proceedings*, 1961, pp. 30-38.

Kerley, Ernest. "The Powers of Investigation of the United Nations Security Council," *American Journal of International Law*, lv (October 1961), 892-918.

Knorr, Klaus, and Sidney Verba (eds.). *The International System: Theoretical Essays*. Princeton: Princeton University Press, 1961.

Komarnicki, Titus. "The Place of Neutrality in the Modern System of International Law," Hague *Recueil des Cours*, 1952.

Lande, Gabriella Rosner. "The Changing Effectiveness of General Assembly Resolutions," American Society of International Law *Proceedings*, 1964, pp. 162-170.

Lansdale, Major-General Edward G. "Vietnam: Do We Understand Revolution," *Foreign Affairs*, xliii (October 1964), 75-86.

Lash, Joseph. "Dag Hammarskjöld's Conception of His Office," *International Organization*, xvi (Summer 1962), 542-566.

Laquer, Walter. "Communism and Nationalism in Tropical Africa," *Foreign Affairs*, xxxix (July 1961), 610-621.

Lauterpacht, Hersch. *International Law and Human Rights*. New York: Praeger, 1950.

Lefever, Ernest. *Crisis in the Congo: A United Nations Force in Action.* Washington: The Brookings Institution, 1965.

Legum, Colin. *Congo Disaster.* Baltimore: Penguin Books, 1961.

————. "What Kind of Radicalism for Africa," *Foreign Affairs,* XLIII (January 1965), 237-251.

Levi, Werner. "On the Causes of War and the Conditions of Peace," *Journal of Conflict-Resolution,* IV (December 1960), 411-425.

Lindsay, Franklin. "Unconventional Warfare," *Foreign Affairs,* XL (January 1962), 264-274.

Lissitzyn, Oliver. "International Law in a Divided World," *International Conciliation,* No. 542, March, 1963.

MacDougal, Myres, and Gerhard Bebr. "Human Rights in the United Nations," *American Journal of International Law,* LVIII (July 1964), 603-641.

MacDougal, Myres, and Florentino Feliciano. *Toward Minimum World Public Order.* New Haven: Yale University Press, 1961.

Marcum, John. "Unilateral Intervention in the Congo and its Political Consequences," American Society of International Law *Proceedings,* 1961, pp. 27-30.

Martin, Laurence (ed.). *Neutralism and Non-Alignment.* New York: Praeger, 1962.

Mazrui, Ali A. "The United Nations and Some African Political Attitudes," *International Organization,* XVIII (Summer 1964), 499-520.

Mendlovitz, Saul (ed.). *Legal and Political Problems of World Order.* New York: The Fund for Education Concerning World Peace Through World Law, 1962.

Methvin, E. H. "Ideology and Organization in Counter-Insurgency," *Orbis,* VII (Spring 1964), 106-124.

Millikan, Max, and Donald Blackmer (eds.). *The Emerging Nations.* Cambridge: Massachusetts Institute of Technology, 1961.

Modelski, George. *The International Relations of Internal War,* Center of International Studies, Research Memorandum No. 9. Princeton: 1961.

Nation-Building: The Order of the Day, Spring 1962 issue of *Journal of International Affairs*, XVI.

Nicholas, Herbert. *The United Nations as a Political Institution*. London: Oxford University Press, 1959.

O'Brien, Conor Cruise. *Conflicting Concepts of the U.N.* Leeds, England: Leeds University Press, 1964.

———. *To Katanga and Back*. New York: Simon and Schuster, 1962.

Osanka, Franklin Mark (ed.). *Modern Guerrilla Warfare*. New York: Free Press of Glencoe, 1962.

Pace, Eric. "Laos: Continuing Crisis," *Foreign Affairs*, XLIII (October 1964), 64-74.

Padelford, Norman. "Financial Crisis and the Future of the United Nations," *World Politics*, XV (July 1963), 531-568.

———. *International Law and Diplomacy in the Spanish Civil Strife*. New York: Macmillan, 1939.

———. "The Organization of African Unity," *International Organization*, XVIII (Summer 1964), 521-542.

Perkins, Whitney T. "Sanctions for Political Change—The Indonesian Case," *International Organization*, XII (Winter 1958), 26-42.

Petersen, Keith. "The Uses of the Uniting For Peace Resolution Since 1950," *International Organization*, XIII (Summer 1959), 219-232.

Preuss, Lawrence. "Article 2:7 of the United Nations Charter and Matters of Domestic Jurisdiction," *Hague Recueil des Cours*, 1949.

Rajan, M. S. *The United Nations and Domestic Jurisdiction*. New York: Asia Publishing House, 1961.

Rosenau, James (ed.). *International Aspects of Civil Strife*. Princeton: Princeton University Press, 1964.

Rosner, Gabriella. *The United Nations Emergency Force*. New York: Columbia University Press, 1963.

Russell, Ruth B. *A History of the United Nations Charter*. Washington: Brookings Institution, 1958.

Sanger, Clyde. "Toward Unity in Africa," *Foreign Affairs*, XLII (January 1964), 269-281.

Schachter, Oscar. "Dag Hammarskjöld and the Relation of

Law to Politics," *American Journal of International Law,* LVI (January 1962), 1-8.

———. "Legal Aspects of U.N. Action in the Congo," *American Journal of International Law,* LV (January 1961), 1-28.

———. "Preventing the Internationalization of Internal Conflict: A Legal Analysis of the U.N. Congo Experience," American Society of International Law *Proceedings,* 1963, pp. 216-224.

Slade, Ruth. *The Belgian Congo.* London: Oxford University Press, 1960.

Sohn, Louis. "The Role of the United Nations in Civil Wars," American Society of International Law *Proceedings,* 1963, pp. 208-215.

Spencer, John. "Africa at the U.N.: Some Observations," *International Organization,* XVI (Spring 1962), 375-386.

Spiro, Herbert J. *Politics in Africa.* Englewood Cliffs: Prentice-Hall, 1964.

Stanger, Roland (ed.). *Essays on Intervention.* Columbus, Ohio: Ohio State University Press, 1964.

Stein, Eric. "Mr. Hammarskjöld, The Charter Law and the Future Role of the United Nations Secretary-General," *American Journal of International Law,* LVI (January 1962), 9-32.

Stoessinger, John, and Associates. *Financing the United Nations System.* Washington: Brookings Institution, 1964.

Stone, Julius. *Aggression and World Order.* Berkeley: University of California Press, 1958.

———. *Legal Controls of International Conflict.* 2nd ed. London: Stevens, 1959.

———. *The Quest for Survival.* Cambridge: Harvard University Press, 1961.

Talarides, Kikes. "Les Aspects Constitutionnels et Internationaux de l'Affaire de Chypre," *Politique Étrangère,* XXIX, No. 1 (1964), 74-91.

Taubenfeld, Howard J., and Rita F. Taubenfeld. "Independent Revenue for the United Nations," *International Organization,* XVIII (Spring 1964), 241-267.

Taylor, Alastair. *Indonesian Independence and the United Nations.* Ithaca: Cornell University Press, 1960.

Travis, Martin. "The Political and Social Bases for the Latin American Doctrine of Non-Intervention," American Society of International Law *Proceedings,* 1959, pp. 68-72.

Tsou, Tang, and Morton H. Halperin. "Mao-Tse-Tung's Revolutionary Strategy and Peking's International Behavior," *American Political Science Review,* LIX (March 1965), 89-99.

Vallat, F. A. "The Competence of the United Nations General Assembly," Hague *Recueil des Cours,* 1959.

Wainhouse, David. *Remnants of Empire: The United Nations and the End of Colonialism.* New York: Harper and Row, 1964.

Waldock, C.H.M. "The Control of the Use of Force by States in International Law," Hague *Recueil des Cours,* 1952.

Wallerstein, Immanuel. *Africa: The Politics of Independence.* New York: Vintage Books, 1961.

West, Robert L. "The United Nations and the Congo Crisis: Lessons of the First Year," *International Organization,* XV (Autumn 1961), 603-617.

Wilcox, Francis O., and H. Field Haviland. *The United States and the United Nations.* Baltimore: Johns Hopkins University Press, 1961.

Wohlgemuth, Patricia. "The Portuguese Territories and the United Nations," *International Conciliation,* No. 545, November, 1963.

Wright, Quincy. *International Law and the United Nations.* Delhi: Asia House, 1960.

——. "Peacekeeping Operations of the U.N.," *International Studies,* VII (October 1965), 169-205.

——. "The Legality of Intervention under the U.N. Charter," American Society of International Law *Proceedings,* 1957, pp. 79-91.

——. *The Role of International Law in the Elimination of War.* Manchester: University of Manchester Press, 1961.

——. "United States Intervention in the Lebanon,"

American Journal of International Law, LIII (January 1959), 112-126.

Young, Crawford. *Politics in the Congo.* Princeton: Princeton University Press, 1965.

Young, Kenneth. "New Politics in New States," *Foreign Affairs,* XXXIX (April 1961), 494-503.

Xydis, Stephen. "America, Britain and the USSR in the Greek Arena, 1944-1947," *Political Science Quarterly,* LXXVIII (December 1963), 581-596.

Index

United Nations Yemen Observation Mission (UNYOM), 122, 187-88

United States, 13, 14, 14n, 16-17, 48, 52n, 55n, 61, 62, 181, 183, 185, 187, 202, 204, 208, 211; and Indonesia, 41-46 *passim*; and Angola, 57, 58, 59; and Congo, 70, 70n, 72n, 75, 75n, 80, 83, 85, 87, 88, 89n, 93, 98-110 *passim*; 112-16 *passim*; and Cyprus, 118, 121, 122, 127, 134, 135, 139, 145, 147; and Dominican Republic, 149-64 *passim*; and Greece, 174-78; and Guatemala, 180-81; and Indochina, 189-200 *passim*

Uniting for Peace Resolution, 29-30, 80

Uruguay, 152, 155, 156, 161, 182, 196

Venezuela, 153

Vietnam, 5, 8, 14, 17, 173, 190-200 *passim*, 202, 203, 206, 211. *See also* Indochina

Wachuku, Jaja, 90, 190

Warsaw Treaty, 181

Wessin, Elias Wessin y, 150, 151, 157

Yemen, 5, 8, 12, 14n, 17, 120, 173, 186-89, 199, 200, 201, 207

Yugoslavia, 174-79 *passim*

Zurich-London agreements, 117, 132, 147

OTHER BOOKS PUBLISHED FOR
THE CENTER OF INTERNATIONAL STUDIES
PRINCETON UNIVERSITY

Gabriel A. Almond, *The Appeals of Communism*
Gabriel A. Almond and James S. Coleman, editors, *The Politics of the Developing Areas*
Gabriel A. Almond and Sidney Verba, *The Civic Culture: Political Attitudes and Democracy in Five Nations*
Richard J. Barnet and Richard A. Falk, *Security in Disarmament*
Cyril E. Black and Thomas P. Thornton, editors, *Communism and Revolution: The Strategic Uses of Political Violence*
Robert J. C. Butow, *Tojo and the Coming of the War*
Miriam Camps, *Britain and the European Community, 1955-1963*
Bernard C. Cohen, *The Political Process and Foreign Policy: The Making of the Japanese Peace Settlement*
Bernard C. Cohen, *The Press and Foreign Policy*
Charles De Visscher, *Theory and Reality in Public International Law*, translated by P. E. Corbett
Frederick S. Dunn, *Peace-making and the Settlement with Japan*
Harry Eckstein, *Division and Cohesion in Democracy: A Study of Norway*
Richard F. Hamilton, *Affluence and the French Worker in the Fourth Republic*
Herman Kahn, *On Thermonuclear War*
W. W. Kaufmann, editor, *Military Policy and National Security*
Klaus Knorr, *On the Uses of Military Power in the Nuclear Age*
Klaus Knorr, *The War Potential of Nations*
Klaus Knorr, editor, *NATO and American Security*
Klaus Knorr and Sidney Verba, editors, *The International System: Theoretical Essays*
Peter Kunstadter, editor, *Southeast Asian Tribes, Minorities, and Nations*
Sidney J. Ploss, *Conflict and Decision-making in Soviet Russia*
Lucian W. Pye, *Guerrilla Communism in Malaya*
James N. Rosenau, editor, *International Aspects of Civil Strife*
James N. Rosenau, *National Leadership and Foreign Policy: A Case Study in the Mobilization of Public Support*
Rolf Sannwald and Jacques Stohler, *Economic Integration: Theoretical Assumptions and Consequences of European Unification.* Translated by Herman F. Karreman
Richard L. Sklar, *Nigerian Political Parties: Power in an Emergent African Nation*
Glenn H. Snyder, *Deterrence and Defense*
Harold and Margaret Sprout, *The Ecological Perspective on Human Affairs, With Special Reference to International Politics*
Thomas P. Thornton, *The Third World in Soviet Perspective: Studies by Soviet Writers on the Developing Areas*
Sidney Verba, *Small Groups and Political Behavior: A Study of Leadership*
Karl von Vorys, *Political Development in Pakistan*
Myron Weiner, *Party Politics in India*
E. Victor Wolfenstein, *The Revolutionary Personality: Lenin, Trotsky, Gandhi*
Oran R. Young, *The Intermediaries: Third Parties in International Crises*

235